EXECUTIVE
ETIQUETTE

CONTEMPORARY ETIQUETTE
AND BUSINESS PRACTICE FOR
THE PROFESSIONAL PERSON

Copyright © 1990 by
Executive Etiquette, Inc.

ALL RIGHTS, INCLUDING THAT OF TRANSLATION, RESERVED. THIS BOOK IS PROTECTED BY COPYRIGHT. NO PART OF THIS BOOK MAY BE REPRODUCED OR TRANSMITTED IN ANY FORM OR BY ANY MEANS, INCLUDING PHOTOCOPYING, OR BY ANY INFORMATION STORAGE AND RETRIEVAL SYSTEM WITHOUT PRIOR WRITTEN PERMISSION FROM D I PUBLICATIONS, INC., EDITORIAL OFFICE, 4720 MONTGOMERY LANE, BETHESDA, MD 20814. NAMES USED IN THIS BOOK ARE FOR ILLUSTRATIVE PURPOSES AND ANY SIMILARITY TO ACTUAL PERSONS OR COMPANIES IS COINCIDENTAL.

Library of Congress Catalog Card Number 90-81919

ISBN 0-914768-49-2

DISTRIBUTED BY
D I PUBLICATIONS, INC.
1241 BROADWAY, HAMILTON, IL 62341 U.S.A.

PRINTED IN THE UNITED STATES OF AMERICA BY
HAMILTON PRESS, INC.

EXECUTIVE
ETIQUETTE

CONTENTS

PREFACE ix

1 COMMUNICATIONS

Business Cards 3
Specifications 3, Purpose 4, Use 5

Business Correspondence 6
Business Documents 6, Stationery 8, Business Letters-Elements 9, Business Letters-Formats 15, Letters of Reference 19, Memoranda-Elements/Formats 20

Conversation 23
What to Say 24, Effective Speaking and Listening 25

Greetings & Introductions 27
Addressing Others 27, Greetings 28, Introductions 29, Forms of Address [Table] 31

Invitations & Replies 36
Types of Invitations 36, Content of Invitations 37, Mailing Invitations 40, Replies 41, Other Responsibilities 41

Presentations/Speaking 43
Preparation 43, Delivery 44, Stage Presence 46, Introducing the Speaker 46

Telecommunication 47
Answering the Telephone 47, Placing a Telephone Call 49, Telephone Conversation 49, Additional Guidelines 50

2 MEETINGS/CONFERENCES

The Meeting Chairperson 53
Pre-Meeting 54, During the Meeting 54, Meeting Notes 55

The Meeting Participants   57
Pre-Meeting 57, During the Meeting 57

Office Appointments   59

Offsite Appointments   60

Job Interviews   60
Interviewer 61, Interviewee 61, Résumé 62

Board of Directors Meetings   64

Conferences   65

3 DINING/ENTERTAINING

Cocktail Functions   69
*Considerations for the Host 69,
Considerations for the Guest 71*

Restaurant Dining Manners   73
*Reservations 73, Arrival and Seating 74,
Ordering 75, Conversation 76, Eating 76,
Receiving the Bill 77, Glossary of Foods 78*

Table Manners   81
*Before the Meal 81, Service of the Meal 82,
Wine Service 83, During the Meal 84,
Toasting 85, Consuming Specific Foods 86*

Table Settings   92
*Flatware 92, Multicourse Place Setting
[Illus.] 94, Holding the Fork [Illus.] 95,
Utensil Placement [Illus.] 95, China 96,
Crystal 97, Condiment Servers 97, Napkins 98, Place/Menu Cards 98, Centerpiece and Candles 99, Seating Arrangements 99, Ranked Seating [Illus.] 100*

4 GIFTS/TRAVEL/COURTESIES

Business Gifts   103
*Giving Office Gifts 103, Receiving Office
Gifts 104, Business Associate Gifts 105*

Business Travel — 106
Preparation 106, In Transit 107, At the Hotel/Dining 108

General Courtesies — 110
Anthem/Flag 110, Doors 111, Elevators 111, Escalators/Moving Walks 112, Rising/Standing 112, Seating 112, Smoking 113, Tipping 113, Walking 115

International Courtesies — 116
General Considerations 116, Japanese Business Style 118

5 PERSONAL GROOMING & BUSINESS DRESS

General Considerations — 121
Grooming 121, Clothing 122, Office Grooming Kit 123

Attire for Women — 123
Businesswear 123, Hosiery/Shoes 124, Accessories/Jewelry 124

Attire for Men — 124
Suits 124, Shirts 125, Neckties 125, Underwear/Socks/Shoes 126, Accessories/Jewelry 126

Attire for Video — 127

INDEX — 129

PREFACE

The ability to relate well with others has always been valued in society, and a knowledge of etiquette provides the basis for a person to develop this quality. Etiquette skills are also important in business, and are often essential if one is to advance professionally.

Etiquette, simply stated, is the combination of good manners with a sincere respect for others. Today's business executive, although highly educated, frequently lacks a sound knowledge of etiquette. This may be coupled with little training in basic business practices. Such deficits not only affect the businessperson's individual performance, but can impact on a firm's overall productivity and company image.

In recent years, the increasingly competitive business environment has led to renewed interest in obtaining guidance in manners and interpersonal dynamics. This interest is recognition that greater etiquette awareness can yield dividends in the form of improved communications and strengthened business relationships.

Executive Etiquette provides the businessperson of the 1990's with a ready source of information on contemporary etiquette and basic business skills. The content and format of the book are designed to facilitate rapid retrieval and understanding of the subject matter. It is the authors' hope that, through use of *Executive Etiquette,* the reader will achieve a more rewarding professional life.

1 · COMMUNICATIONS

BUSINESS CARDS

BUSINESS CORRESPONDENCE

CONVERSATION

GREETINGS & INTRODUCTIONS

INVITATIONS & REPLIES

PRESENTATIONS/SPEAKING

TELECOMMUNICATION

Virtually every aspect of business life involves both written and verbal communication. Effective interpersonal and organizational communications are vital to the proper functioning of a company and the promotion of its corporate image. This Chapter provides guidance in business communications.

BUSINESS CARDS

A well designed business card is essential for the business or professional person. The card provides a means by which you are remembered by the recipient, so the card should reflect quality in every respect.

Specifications

Generally, a business card is conservative in design, although innovative designs with a quality look may also be acceptable. The card should conform to the standard size of three and one-half by two inches, allowing it to fit into a business card holder. The overall appearance, texture and color of card stock, and print characteristics are critical and should be carefully selected. The following print characteristics should be considered: the color of print; font (kind, style, and size of type); and whether the card is printed, engraved, thermographed (raised print), embossed (the image is in relief, with or without ink), or some combination thereof.

Business cards are designed in many different styles. Usually, a company logo is located along the top of the card. Your name, academic/professional degree (if applicable), and position are centered. The business name can be located at the top, or in the lower left or right corner. The business address is placed in the lower left or right corner, with the telephone number in the opposite corner. For sales staff, the business name and address will often be centered, with the salesperson's name and position in the lower left and telephone number in the lower right corner.

4 EXECUTIVE ETIQUETTE

Note that Mr., Ms., Miss, and Mrs. titles are not used on business cards (in contrast to social cards), unless the first name could be confused as male or female. If well established, a nickname may be included; for example, John ("Jack") Doe.

The following are examples:

STEPHEN R. McNEIL
ATTORNEY AT LAW

LAW OFFICES OF
LEVIN, SHRIVER & CHEN
1500 K STREET, SUITE 725
WASHINGTON, DC 20005   (202) 555-1212

MEDCOM
INCORPORATED

MEDICAL COMMUNICATIONS, INC.
1100 CENTURY BLVD.
LOS ANGELES, CA 90080

ANNE M. HUNTLEY, M.S.
GOVERNMENT ACCOUNTS   (213) 555-1212

Purpose

The business card is properly used:

- To give business or professional identification informa-

tion to another individual, such as a business contact, colleague, client or sales prospect.
- As a cover attachment to documents being sent to others, to identify the sender.
- As an enclosure with a gift, to identify the sender.
- Occasionally, to serve as a medium for brief messages.

Use

A few guidelines should be followed in the use of business cards:

- Provide your card to those who have shown an interest in receiving or exchanging such information.
- If someone gives you their business card, promptly reciprocate with a card of your own.
- Do not offer your card to unknown persons you happen to meet or those who are superior in rank, unless there is evident interest in receiving your card.
- Provide only crisp, clean, and up-to-date cards.
- Do not leave a pile of cards or scatter them about at a meeting or other gathering.
- Do not offer your card at a strictly social event, and never during a meal.
- When used as an attachment or enclosure, it is preferable that you write a note on the front or back (write "over" on the front) of the card. If the recipient is someone you know well, line out the printed name and sign your given name.
- For close friends and those who are ill, a gift card or personal note is preferred as an enclosure with flowers or a gift.

Business cards have an importance that far outweighs their minimal cost. You should not scrimp on this aspect of your business.

BUSINESS CORRESPONDENCE

The impression of you as an individual and the firm you represent will be made by both the form and content of your written communication. Business correspondence which is properly formatted, grammatically correct and which effectively conveys your thoughts is an important component of business success. Not only is the ability to write well a valuable asset, it is often essential in today's complex business environment.

Business Documents

Purpose.
Types of business documents include business letters, letters of reference, internal memoranda, notes and reports. While the substance of these documents varies, all serve the purpose of communicating thought. That thought may be to inform, to request information, initiate action or to record an event.

Composition.
Written communications should always be logically constructed, keeping in mind the purpose and intent of the communication. An outline is very useful in organizing your thoughts—concepts may be arranged from the most important to least important, chronologically, or in some other logical sequence. Whatever approach is used, the outline should begin with the purpose of the communication and lead to a clear conclusion, recommendation or call for action. A determination should be made about the need

for a review of background material or research on the subject, and this task accomplished before proceeding further; the outline is then revised accordingly. A written draft of the communication is prepared using the outline as a guide. State the most important points early, and provide any supporting material. Sentences should be clear and concise, grammatically correct and have no spelling errors. Word selection and usage are important—a conversational style is considered best, avoiding multisyllabic or overly technical terms and stilted phraseology.

The written draft should be reviewed and revised as often as necessary until it is satisfactory.

A critical aspect of any document, particularly correspondence, is the tone it conveys. For example, a business letter which has a professional *and* friendly tone is generally better received and more effective in achieving its intended objective. All documents should convey a sense of credibility and an interest in the reader's perspective.

Appearance.
The overall appearance of a business document has an immediate impact on the reader's perception of the sender and may also influence how the message is received. Factors which combine to form a document's appearance include the stationery used; neatness of typing; standard elements which comprise the document; formatting of the elements and positioning of the text on the page. The use of text embellishments such as character bolding or headings (e.g., "Background") in memoranda and reports also enhance the appearance as well as readability of such documents.

The guidelines which follow focus on accepted business practices in the preparation of business letters and memoranda.

Stationery

Letterhead.
Factors to consider in selecting stationery include paper and print characteristics, logo design and layout of the letterhead, all of which combine to form an image of the firm. Paper should be high quality bond in standard sizes (8 1/2" x 11" Standard Business; and 7 1/4" x 10 1/2" Executive or Monarch), with attention given to the basis weight (20 or 24 lb.), rag or cotton fiber content (25 or 50%), texture and color. Print font (kind, style and size of type) and ink color are also important considerations. The logo, lettering of the letterhead or memoranda headers and envelope address may be printed, engraved, thermographed (raised print), or embossed (the image is in relief, with or without ink), or some combination thereof. For most companies, paper and print selections tend to be conservative and layout of the letterhead presents a balanced appearance, although a carefully designed contemporary look may also be effectively employed. Letterhead will normally include the company's logo, name, address and telephone number. It may also include an organizational unit within the firm; the writer's office or name and position, located in the upper left corner; names of principals of the firm; cable address and/or FAX telephone number. Paper used for continuation sheets and envelopes should match that used for the letterhead sheet.

Envelopes.
Standard business letter envelopes include Commercial No. 6 3/4 (3 5/8" x 6 1/2", which requires three folds of the letter to fit into the envelope) and, more commonly, No. 10 (4 1/8" x 9 1/2", requiring two parallel folds). Envelopes for Executive/Monarch size paper are 3 7/8" x 7 1/2", requiring two parallel folds of the letter. The firm's name and address are printed on the front, upper left corner of the envelope.

Business Letters - Elements

The standard elements of a business letter are discussed below in order of appearance; all elements are normally separated by at least two spaces. A composite sample letter is shown in Figure 1, page 14.

Date Line.
Normally, the date line is placed three to seven lines below the letterhead, taking into account the overall length of the letter. The month should be spelled out (i.e., no Arabic numerals or abbreviations). The sequence of month-day-year, with a comma between the day and year, is standard; some offices, such as in the military, may use the sequence of day-month-year without punctuation (e.g., 15 July 1990).

Declarations/Notations.
Special mailing declarations and on-arrival notations should be placed flush with the left margin on succeeding lines, entirely capitalized. For example:

REGISTERED MAIL
CONFIDENTIAL

Inside Address.
An inside address to an individual should begin with the person's personal or professional title (Mr., Ms., Miss, Mrs., Dr., etc.) and full name. If an academic or professional degree is placed after the name, a preceding personal or professional title is unnecessary. The person's business title/position, business division (if needed) and name, and the business address follow on succeeding lines (a short business title and division can be placed on the same line, such as "Director, Sales Unit"). If the letter is addressed to a company, the business name, division and business address are provided. Other than personal or professional titles and degrees, abbreviations should be avoid-

ed. Numbered street names from one to twelve are usually spelled out (such as 230 First Street), with Arabic numerals (and, optionally, "st," "nd," "rd," "th") used for street names over twelve. When the building and street numbers are both figures, separate them with a spaced hyphen (such as 230 - 70th Street). Use the Postal Service's two letter abbreviation for the state. Always single space within the inside address.

Attention Line.
When an attention line is used to bring the letter to the attention of a particular individual within the company, "Attention:" is usually used plus the person's personal or professional title and full name (and division if needed).

Salutation.
The salutation "Dear" plus a person's personal or professional title and surname is standard. You may also use "Dear" and the person's given name if you are on a first name basis (if using form letters, line out the person's typed surname and write in his/her given name). For high level persons, use proper forms of address—see the table in the Section entitled "Greetings & Introductions." If the letter is addressed to a company generally, the salutation "Dear Sir or Madam," "Dear Madam or Sir" or "Ladies and Gentlemen" may be used. If the company is known to be comprised of only men or only women, "Gentlemen" or "Ladies" is used, respectively. When an attention line is employed, the salutation still conforms to the addressee which is the company; in other words, use "Dear Sir or Madam" or "Ladies and Gentlemen."

Subject Line.
A subject line may be placed before or after the salutation. Preceding words such as "Subject:", "Reference:", "RE:", "Re:" or "In re:" can be used. The entire line may be capitalized or underlined for emphasis.

Text.
The text is normally single spaced, with double spacing between paragraphs. For brief letters, one and one-half or double spacing can be used within a paragraph, with either paragraph indentation or triple spacing between paragraphs. To provide emphasis or to accommodate lengthy item enumerations or quotations, such material should be entirely indented by blocking it at least five spaces from both the left and right margins.

A minimum of two or three lines of text should be carried over to warrant a continuation sheet. There are various formats used for the heading of continuation pages; among these are to:

- Place the page number with spaced hyphens either flush with the left margin or centered:

- 2 -

- Place the addressee's personal/professional title and full name flush with the left margin, and center the page number with spaced hyphens (and, optionally, place the letter date flush with the right margin):

Mr. Arnold E. Kearns - 2 - July 15, 1990

- Place the page number, a spaced hyphen, and the addressee's personal/professional title and full name flush with the left margin:

Page 2 - Mr. Arnold E. Kearns

- Or, place the page number and the addressee's title and full name in either order and, optionally, letter date, flush with the left margin on succeeding lines:

Page 2	*or*	Mr. Arnold E. Kearns
Mr. Arnold E. Kearns		Page 2
July 15, 1990		July 15, 1990

Complimentary Close.
There are many possible closes for a business letter, ranging from the formal to the informal or personal. Some examples of these follow.

Formal:	Very respectfully; Respectfully yours; Respectfully; Very truly yours; Yours very truly; Yours truly.
Less Formal:	Very sincerely yours; Very sincerely; Most sincerely; Sincerely yours; Yours sincerely; Sincerely.
Informal:	Cordially yours; Yours cordially; Most cordially; Cordially; Kindest regards; Best regards; Regards; Best wishes.

Signature Block.
The writer's full name, degree (if applicable), business title/position, and the business division (if needed) is standard. Any of this information which appears in the letterhead may be omitted from the signature block. Normally, the company name is not typed in the signature block; however, if the company name is not present in the letterhead, it may be typed after the writer's name and position (see Figure 7, page 18). Some firms employ a modified format, particularly where the writer is speaking "for the company;" the company name is placed two lines beneath the complimentary close and is entirely capitalized:

>Sincerely yours,
>
>SMITH & COMPANY
>*<SIGNATURE>*
>(Mrs.) Maria Fenton, C.P.A.
>Director, Escrow Department.

Space permitting, signature block information may be placed on the same line ("Harry J. Smith, President"). The signature block is aligned vertically with the complimentary close, and placed three to five lines below the complimentary close to allow adequate space for the writer's signature. Womens' marital status titles which precede, and degrees or certifications which follow, the writer's name in the signature block are not included in the person's written signature. The writer may sign the letter with only his given name, if the salutation is in the same form. If a person who is not the writer signs the letter, he should legibly sign his own name, followed by "for."

Closing Data.
The initials of the letter writer and typist, separated with a colon or diagonal (/), may be indicated. Commonly, the writer's initials will be omitted and many companies now place all such identifier data (including the name or initials of the person who drafted the letter, if different from the signer) only on the office file copy of the letter.

Enclosures or attachments are indicated next. The number or a list of enclosed/attached items may be specified (e.g., Enc. (3), Encl. (3), Attachments - 3).

The carbon copy notation "cc:" or "Copy to:" is indicated next and, on the same line, the first recipient name is listed; other recipient names are aligned with the first name on succeeding lines. The blind carbon copy notation "bcc:"—used when the writer does not want the distribution list on the addressee's letter—is placed in the same position on only the file and bcc recipient copies of the letter.

Envelope Address.
The envelope address should normally match the inside address of the letter. Special mailing declarations are entirely capitalized and placed beneath the postage. On-

14 EXECUTIVE ETIQUETTE

arrival notations are entirely capitalized and placed midway, flush left or diagonally, between the return address and the recipient's mailing address.

FIGURE 1. COMPOSITE SAMPLE LETTER

SMITH & COMPANY
4350 STATE STREET
BETHESDA, MARYLAND 20814
(301) 555-1212

July 15, 1990

CERTIFIED MAIL

Georgetown Partnership, Ltd.
5700 Oakdale Avenue
Bethesda, MD 20814

Attention: Mr. Arnold E. Kearns

Gentlemen:

RE: Bethesda Park Office Building

We are in receipt of your certified check number 300, in the amount of $178,500.00, as a deposit to the escrow account for the Bethesda Park Office Building located at 7100 Wisconsin Avenue, Bethesda, Maryland. A deposit receipt is enclosed.

Thank you.

> Sincerely yours,
>
> *<SIGNATURE>*
> Harry J. Smith
> President

Enclosure

Business Letters - Formats

There are several accepted formats for preparing a business letter. The following are brief descriptions of the forms commonly in use.

Full Block Form [Figure 2].

In the Full Block Form of a letter, all elements (discussed previously) are begun flush with the left margin and are separated with at least double spacing.

FIGURE 2. FULL BLOCK FORM

> SMITH & COMPANY
> 4350 STATE STREET
> BETHESDA, MARYLAND 20814
> (301) 555-1212

July 15, 1990

Mr. Arnold E. Kearns
5700 Oakdale Avenue
Bethesda, MD 20814

Dear Mr. Kearns:

We are in receipt of your certified check number 300,...

Sincerely yours,
<SIGNATURE>
Harry J. Smith
President

Modified Block Form [Figure 3].

The Modified Block Form follows the Full Block Form, except that the date line, complimentary close and signature block begin at the center or to the right-of-center of the page.

16 EXECUTIVE ETIQUETTE

FIGURE 3. MODIFIED BLOCK FORM

July 15, 1990

Mr. Arnold E. Kearns
5700 Oakdale Avenue
Bethesda, MD 20814

Dear Mr. Kearns:

We are in receipt of your certified check number 300,...

                        Sincerely yours,
                        <SIGNATURE>
                        Harry J. Smith
                        President

Modified Semiblock Form [Figure 4].

This Form follows the Modified Block Form, except that the first word of each paragraph of the text is indented five to seven spaces.

FIGURE 4. MODIFIED SEMIBLOCK FORM

July 15, 1990

Mr. Arnold E. Kearns
5700 Oakdale Avenue
Bethesda, MD 20814

Dear Mr. Kearns:

     We are in receipt of your certified check number...

                        Sincerely yours,
                        <SIGNATURE>
                        Harry J. Smith
                        President

Simplified Form [Figure 5].
The Simplified Form follows the Full Block Form, but replaces the salutation with a capitalized subject line; eliminates the complimentary close; and capitalizes the writer's name and title.

<u>**FIGURE 5. SIMPLIFIED FORM**</u>

July 15, 1990

Mr. Arnold E. Kearns
5700 Oakdale Avenue
Bethesda, MD 20814

RECEIPT OF DEPOSIT CHECK

We are in receipt of your certified check number 300,...

<SIGNATURE>
HARRY J. SMITH, PRESIDENT

Executive Letter Form [Figures 6 and 7].
This Form is used with Executive or Monarch size paper, and is a variation of the Modified Semiblock Form. The inside address, although flush with the left margin, is placed below the signature/signature block. If plain Executive paper is used, the writer's address and then the date are placed in the upper right corner.

Punctuation.
Punctuation is commonly employed as shown in the sample letters: the ends of the date line, inside address lines (unless an abbreviation such as Corp. completes the line) and signature block line(s) are unpunctuated; the salutation is punctuated with a colon; and the complimentary close is punctuated with a comma. With respect to capitalization, except for titles and proper names, only the first letter of the first

18 EXECUTIVE ETIQUETTE

word of the salutation and complimentary close are capitalized.

FIGURE 6. EXECUTIVE FORM [LETTERHEAD]

<LETTERHEAD>

Harry J. Smith
President

July 15, 1990

Dear Mr. Kearns:

    We are in receipt of your certified check number...

Sincerely yours,
<SIGNATURE>

Mr. Arnold E. Kearns
5700 Oakdale Avenue
Bethesda, MD 20814

FIGURE 7. EXECUTIVE FORM [PLAIN PAPER]

4350 State Street
Bethesda, MD 20814

July 15, 1990

Dear Mr. Kearns:

    We are in receipt of your certified check number...

Sincerely yours,
<SIGNATURE>
Harry J. Smith, President
Smith & Company

Mr. Arnold E. Kearns
5700 Oakdale Avenue
Bethesda, MD 20814

Inserting Letter into Envelope.
The proper method of inserting a letter into a No. 10 business or an Executive size envelope is as follows. Fold the bottom third of the letter up; then, fold the top third of the letter down, such that the paper's top edge meets the bottom edge of the bottom fold. The folded letter is then inserted into the envelope, facing the back side of the envelope, so that the recipient need not turn the letter over when it is removed and unfolded.

Letters of Reference

Although prospective employers will often telephone to request information about a business colleague who is applying for a position, it is also common to be asked for a letter of reference. While there is a tendency to provide enthusiastic endorsement of an individual, such a request carries with it the responsibility to be truthful. A colleague who initiates the request for a reference letter directly or by recommending you to the prospective employer will be anticipating a favorable write-up. If you are unable to write a favorable recommendation, your letter may be neutral in tone rather than negative, but you should also consider declining the request.

Letters of reference are of obvious importance, so enough time should be allowed to write an accurate, well organized and professional letter. When developing the letter, note your business relationship with the individual. Review the person's professional attributes, capabilities and character strengths, and provide information which supports your appraisal. Include personal data, if appropriate. Although you may not want to specify an individual's weaknesses in the letter, you should keep them in mind so that the letter will be written with more balance. Note your availability to be contacted for further information, and inform the colleague when the letter is sent.

Memoranda - Elements/Formats

The interoffice memorandum provides an efficient means of transmitting information to others in a company. Like a business letter, the memorandum should be thoughtfully constructed and have a professional tone. The content of the memorandum, however, may be less formal and more to the point than a business letter. Because the recipient of a memorandum will normally be familiar with the subject area, the writer has the latitude to be relatively brief and to include company jargon and technical terms with the assurance of being understood.

Appearance.
As with a business letter, the appearance of an interoffice memorandum can have an immediate impact on how the writer and his message are perceived. Thus, care should be taken in preparing memoranda which are perused by one's colleagues. Memoranda should be neatly typed, properly formatted and present a balanced appearance on the page.

A memorandum may be prepared on plain paper or, more commonly, on forms with preprinted headers. A word processor may also be programmed to generate the memorandum headers on plain bond with the appearance of a preprinted form, in addition to printing the text of the memorandum. Normally, the letterhead has the word "Memorandum" or "Memo;" company name, division or branch office (if needed); and the standard headers of "Date:", "To:", "From:" and "Subject:" which may vary in arrangement on the page.

Elements.
Methods of completing the header information will differ among offices. As with the business letter, the month should be spelled out, with the sequence of month-day-year standard. Usually, the recipient's name (including, op-

tionally, personal or professional titles/degrees, as applicable) and business title/position are given on the "To" line(s). If there are multiple recipients, their names may be listed on the "To" and succeeding lines. Alternatively, "Distribution List" or "See Below" may be placed after "To:" and recipient names listed after a carbon copy notation (cc:) at the bottom of the page; or, "Addressee" may be placed after "To:" and recipient names listed after "Addressees:" at the bottom of the page.

The writer's name and business title are placed after the "From" line(s); he then initials either the "From" line or the signature block where his initials may be typed. Alternatively, only the writer's business title is given on the "From" line, and the writer's full name and titles/degrees are typed in a signature block at the end of the memorandum, where he signs his name.

Format.
Overall alignment of the text below the headers may be flush with the left margin or in vertical alignment with the first letters of the header information. The format for preparing the memorandum may follow the full block, modified or modified semiblock form.

In contrast to a business letter, there is usually no salutation or complimentary close, although closing statements such as "Thank you for your attention to this matter" may be used.

Types of Memoranda.
There are also specialized types of memoranda, such as the issue memorandum and policy memorandum. These often have prescribed formats which are established by the company. An issue memorandum, for example, might include sections entitled Issue/Problem, Background, Current Status, Discussion/Analysis, Summary, and Recommendations.

22 EXECUTIVE ETIQUETTE

Figure 8 presents a sample memorandum.

<u>**FIGURE 8. COMPOSITE SAMPLE MEMORANDUM**</u>

Memorandum SMITH & COMPANY
BETHESDA OFFICE

DATE : September 1, 1990

TO : See Below

FROM : President

SUBJ. : Account Review/Bethesda Park Office Bldg.

> It is anticipated that there will be closure on the subject property within 45 days.
>
> Please review all records pertaining to this property and send me an audit report by September 15, 1990. Thank you.
>
> *<SIGNATURE>*
> Harry J. Smith

cc: Maria Fenton, Escrow Dept.
   Kenneth R. Lehrer, Sales Dept.
   Paul C. Thompson, Legal Dept.

CONVERSATION

"There can be no doubt that of all the accomplishments prized in modern society, that of being agreeable in conversation is the very first. ...It is agreed among us that people must meet frequently, both men and women, and that not only is it agreeable to talk, but that it is a matter of common courtesy to say something, even when there is hardly anything to say."

> From the Introduction to *The Principles of the Art of Conversation,* by J.P. Mahaffy, 1891.

Effective communication in business and the professions is essential to success. Most communication is verbal, involving both the art of speaking and of listening, utilizing words as the primary medium. Words can have many meanings but, if they are properly communicated and received, mutual understanding will occur. Other factors enter into verbal communication, however, and include the pitch, tone, volume and inflection of your voice; nonverbal forms of communication such as body language; and the perception which the listener places on the message. In other words, how you say (and when listening, how you interpret) the spoken word can be as important as what is actually stated. Business leaders who are cognizant of these factors tend to be more adept in their business dealings as a result.

Those persons who also have a good conversational style have an added advantage—they can move through business and nonbusiness subjects with greater ease, making themselves more interesting and therefore more closely listened to by others.

24 EXECUTIVE ETIQUETTE

The following are some of the factors which can lead to more effective conversational skills.

What to Say

A person can develop good conversational skills through some effort and attention to what one says. Such a person is one who speaks easily and confidently, because he/she is truly interested in other people and in life events, and is sensitive to the impact of his statements on other persons.

- Be conversant on a range of topics. Stay current with business, political and social events. Read local, state and national periodicals such as newspapers, news magazines, specialty publications (e.g., environmental newsletter, stock exchange report). Learn about a few areas indepth, including avocational topics. As long as the subjects are not too emotion-laden or beyond ordinary comprehension or interest, they can be a stimulant to conversation.
- Show interest in others. For example, introduce a subject that relates to a person's work; discuss a topic about which he may have a personal interest (e.g., collecting, sailing); or ask in a general sense about his family. Discuss topics in which you and the other person might have a common interest.
- Compliment others on their appearance or abilities, and congratulate them for their achievements; in all cases, be sincere. Acknowledge any compliments you receive graciously.
- Use occasional humor—this is often appreciated.
- Use small talk effectively. Small talk usually involves polite, noncommittal conversations, and is employed to open or restart communication between persons, fill awkward moments of silence, and to serve as a needed diversionary respite between or following business dis-

cussions and particularly demanding meetings.
- Avoid discussions on topics that are generally "off limits." For example: questioning an older person about his age; personally intrusive subjects; controversial subjects which might lead to emotionally heated disagreement; recitations concerning a problem(s); discussions about health or personal tragedy; unflattering or injurious gossip; and offensive or tasteless jokes and statements.

Effective Speaking and Listening

The effectiveness in conveying your thoughts can depend, to a significant extent, on the speaking tools you employ and conversational etiquette you show towards others. For instance:

- Articulate words with an agreeable pitch, tonal quality, tempo or rate of speech, and volume of sound. Give expression to the words through appropriate variations in these vocal characteristics, so that real interest in the subject is evident to the listener. Avoid contrived speech characteristics.
- Use proper grammar and a good working vocabulary that is conversational, natural and suited to your style. Avoid the following: filler words such as "uh" or "you know;" slang or words that are of passing fashion; technical jargon; profanity; prejudicial ethnic or religious terms; and words that are considered sexist.
- Think before you speak. Do not place another person in an uncomfortable position by what you say. Be mindful of the timing and appropriateness of subject matter, in terms of both the context of the conversation and who you are speaking with. Be alert to signs of boredom in listeners and adjust accordingly. Do not dominate a conversation.

- Show interest in speaking and listening through good body language. Always greet others with a firm handshake. Stand or sit with posture comfortably erect. Give complete attention to those with whom you are conversing—maintain good eye contact, avoid the "glazed" eye look or allowing your eyes to wander.
- Maintain good listening habits through concentration on the *thought* being conveyed. Take account of the speaker's choice of words and gestures used in conveying the thought. Occasionally, a deficient speaker or uninteresting subject will place impediments to effective listening. However, the effective listener overcomes these barriers by recognizing his responsibility to be attentive to the speaker and what could be potentially important information. A method of enhancing one's interest and displaying it to the speaker is to make listening responses such as nodding affirmatively and asking questions.
- Do not interrupt others who are speaking with corrections of their grammar, injection of words or phrases the speaker is searching for (unless it is apparent that the speaker needs assistance), or with the finish to a speaker's story.

GREETINGS & INTRODUCTIONS

Upon first meeting someone, the impression you convey impacts significantly on your future relationship. It is therefore important in dealing with business associates and clients that you greet and address them, and make introductions cordially and properly.

Addressing Others

As a general rule, persons whom you first meet should be addressed with the title Mr., Ms., Miss, Mrs. or Dr. (or other rank or professional title such as Commander, Reverend, Senator, etc.) and their surname (last name), noting that Ms. should not be used with a woman's married name (e.g., Ms. Andrea Sullivan, not Ms. James Sullivan). Thereafter, you should continue to address the person in this manner until he/she states that you should use his given (first) name, or you become familiar enough with each other that use of the first name is acceptable.

Within most organizations today, first names are utilized among employees, with a title and person's last name reserved for more senior persons, by age or executive rank. Some firms want to maintain a more formal office environment (and corporate image), however, and prefer that staff address one another by title and last name. If you see a senior colleague who is accompanied by an outside businessperson, you should address that colleague by title and his last name, even if you are ordinarily on a first name basis in the office. The terms "sir" and "ma'am" are considered an outmoded form of verbal address in business.

"Madam" and "Madame," however, are appropriate as a title in officialdom (e.g., "Madam Chairman/Chairperson") and in addressing untitled women who are citizens of another country, respectively. Refer to the table "Forms of Address" in this Section for a listing of proper forms of verbal and written address.

Greetings

You should always rise, step toward a visitor and remain standing when greeting or being introduced to that person. Similarly, when other than your co-workers, you should stand and welcome all visitors and senior company officials to your office.

Greet the other person cordially, with a pleasant demeanor. If you already know the person, something such as "How are you doing?" is said, and you may want to shake hands. Unless you are close personal friends, limit your response to something like "Fine, thanks, and you?" even if you are not doing very well. When being introduced to someone new, offer your hand in a comfortably firm handshake—a man need not wait for a woman to first offer her hand, as was previously the custom. If the palm of your hand is moist, subtly wipe it dry before a handshake. Ordinarily, a glove is removed prior to shaking hands.

After introductions are made, persons should say a few words of greeting to one another, such as "Hello," "How do you do?" "It's nice to meet you," or "I'm very glad to meet you, Mr. Richmond." Generally, greetings that involve hugging or kissing are to be avoided in the office setting. A few pleasantries help to relax everyone, and any business should be initiated only after all participants have been seated and given a few minutes to become accustomed to the surroundings.

Introductions

Whether at a meeting or social function, it is normally the host's responsibility (or that of the executive who arranges a meeting) to greet and introduce people. If a person's name is not clearly heard, you should ask that the name be repeated; and, if the host errs in introducing you, it is usually a good idea to affably correct the mistake. Always introduce an acquaintance whom only you know, if that person is with you or joins you during a group conversation. When introducing a spouse, use his/her first name (e.g., "Dr. Walsh, I would like you to meet my husband, Jim").

If you forget a person's name while making introductions and that person does not introduce himself, apologetically (but without embarrassment) admit your lapse of recall. If you perceive that a person making introductions has forgotten your name or you are not introduced, you should introduce yourself to the others present.

The proper manner of making business introductions can be remembered if a few guidelines are kept in mind. You should introduce:

- a younger person *to* an older person;
- a lower ranking person *to* a higher ranking person;
- a business colleague *to* an outside associate;
- a family member *to* a business colleague/associate;
- all else being equal, a man *to* a woman.

Some examples will illustrate these guidelines. The simplest method is to employ the specified sequence in the guideline with the preposition "to."

> "Mr. Richmond, may I introduce you *to* Dr. David Walsh, Executive Vice-President of the firm. Mr. Richmond is our new Director of Training."

"Mr. Richmond, I would like to introduce you *to* Dr. Walsh, Executive Vice-President of the firm. Mr. Richmond is our new Director of Training."

Alternatively, reverse the guideline sequence and omit the preposition "to."

"Dr. Walsh, may I introduce Mr. John Richmond, our new Director of Training."

"Dr. Walsh, I would like you to meet Mr. John Richmond, our new Director of Training."

"Dr. Walsh, this is our new Director of Training, Mr. John Richmond. Mr. Richmond (or, John), this is Dr. David Walsh, Executive Vice-President of the firm."

As shown in the above examples, it is important to provide descriptive information about a person when making the introductions.

Introductions in a receiving line are the responsibility of the host, the guest who is queued in the waiting line, and/or a staff person assigned to facilitate introductions. At larger functions, when as a guest you may not be readily known by the host, you should introduce yourself, giving your name and identifier information (e.g., position in the firm; company affiliation). If a staff person is assisting, he will greet you, take your name and introduce you to the host (who, in turn, will introduce you to the next person receiving you or the special guest of honor, if present). As the host, you should greet guests with a smile, a warm handshake and a pleasant remark.

Proper forms of address to use in introducing certain persons are given in the following table.

FORMS OF ADDRESS

PERSON	ADDRESS/INTRODUCTION	SALUTATION	CONVERSATION
GOVERNMENT OFFICIALS*			
Federal			
President	The President The White House	Dear Mr. President	Mr. President *or* Sir
Vice-President	The Vice-President Old Executive Office Building	Dear Mr. Vice-President	Mr. Vice-President *or* Sir
Attorney General	The Honorable David Clark Attorney General	Dear Mr. Attorney General *or* Dear Sir	Mr. Attorney General *or* Mr./Attorney General Clark
Cabinet Member	The Honorable David Clark Secretary of Education	Dear Mr. Secretary *or* Dear Sir	Mr. Secretary *or* Mr./Secretary Clark
Senator	The Honorable David Clark U.S. Senate	Dear Senator Clark *or* Dear Sir	Senator *or* Senator Clark
Representative	The Honorable David Clark U.S. House of Representatives	Dear Mr. Clark *or* Dear Sir	Mr. Clark *or* Representative Clark
House Speaker	The Honorable David Clark Speaker of the House of Representatives	Dear Mr. Speaker *or* Dear Sir	Mr. Speaker *or* Mr. Clark
Chief Justice	The Chief Justice The Supreme Court	Dear Mr. Chief Justice *or* Dear Sir	Mr. Chief Justice *or* Sir
Associate Justice	Mr. Justice Clark The Supreme Court	Dear Mr. Justice *or* Dear Justice Clark; Dear Sir	Mr. Justice *or* Justice Clark; Sir
Ambassador	The Honorable David Clark American Ambassador	Dear Mr. Ambassador *or* Dear Amb. Clark; Dear Sir	Mr. Ambassador *or* Amb. Clark; Mr. Clark; Sir

GREETINGS & INTRODUCTIONS 31

32 EXECUTIVE ETIQUETTE

PERSON	ADDRESS/INTRODUCTION	SALUTATION	CONVERSATION
GOVERNMENT OFFICIALS* (Cont'd.)			
State/Local			
Governor	The Honorable David Clark Governor of Rhode Island	Dear Governor *or* Dear Gov. Clark; Dear Sir	Governor *or* Governor Clark; Sir
Senator	The Honorable David Clark Rhode Island Senate	Dear Senator Clark *or* Dear Sir	Senator *or* Senator Clark; Sir
Mayor	The Honorable David Clark Mayor of Newport	Dear Mr. Mayor *or* Mayor Clark; Dear Sir	Mr. Mayor *or* Mayor Clark; Your Honor
Judge	The Honorable David Clark Judge, Superior Court	Dear Judge Clark	Mr. Justice *or* Judge Clark

* - Substitute "Madam" in place of "Mr." or "Sir" for a woman official.

MILITARY PERSONNEL

In the Army, Air Force and Marine Corps, all commissioned officers are addressed by the title of their rank; and all Generals are addressed as "General," both Colonels as "Colonel," and both Lieutenants as "Lieutenant." All Navy, Coast Guard and Public Health Service officers are similarly addressed; and all Admirals are addressed as "Admiral," and both Commanders as "Commander;" officers below the rank of Commander, however, are addressed as "Mister" (i.e., Mr., Ms.). Warrant officers of all services are addressed as "Mister." All chaplains are addressed as "Chaplain;" however, Catholic chaplains, and those Episcopal chaplains who indicate a preference, may be addressed as "Father." In all services, doctors below the rank of General or Admiral may be addressed as "Doctor." Enlisted personnel with ranks of corporal or above (staff sergeant or above in the Air Force, and Chief petty officers in the Navy) are addressed by their titles. All other enlisted personnel are addressed by their last names. For example:

General	General Louis Bradley, USMC	Dear General Bradley	General Bradley *or* General
Colonel	Lt. Colonel Louis Bradley, USA	Dear Colonel Bradley	Colonel Bradley *or* Colonel
Lieutenant	Lieutenant Louis Bradley, USN	Dear Mr. Bradley	Mr. Bradley *or* Lieutenant

GREETINGS & INTRODUCTIONS 33

Corresponding commissioned officer ranks among the uniformed services are as follows:

Army/Air Force/Marine Corps	Navy/Coast Guard/Public Health Service
General	Admiral
Lieutenant General	Vice Admiral
Major General	Rear Admiral [upperhalf]
Brigadier General	Rear Admiral [lowerhalf]
Colonel	Captain
Lieutenant Colonel	Commander
Major	Lieutenant Commander
Captain	Lieutenant
First Lieutenant	Lieutenant [Junior Grade]
Second Lieutenant	Ensign

PERSON	ADDRESS/INTRODUCTION	SALUTATION	CONVERSATION
PROFESSIONAL PERSONS			
Architect	Joan Palmer, A.I.A.	Dear Ms. Palmer	Ms. Palmer
Attorney	Joan Palmer, J.D., Attorney at Law	Dear Dr. Palmer	Dr. Palmer
	or Joan Palmer, Esq.	Dear Ms. Palmer	Ms. Palmer
Dentist	Joan Palmer, D.D.S.	Dear Dr. Palmer	Dr. Palmer
Optometrist	Joan Palmer, O.D.	Dear Dr. Palmer	Dr. Palmer
Pharmacist	Joan Palmer, Pharm.D.	Dear Dr. Palmer	Dr. Palmer
Physician	Joan Palmer, M.D. (or D.O.)	Dear Dr. Palmer	Dr. Palmer
Professor	Joan Palmer, Ph.D.	Dear Dr. Palmer	Dr. Palmer
	Professor of Political Science	*or* Dear Professor Palmer	*or* Professor Palmer

34 EXECUTIVE ETIQUETTE

PERSON	ADDRESS/INTRODUCTION	SALUTATION	CONVERSATION
RELIGIOUS PERSONS			
Jewish			
Rabbi	Rabbi Richard Halpern	Dear Rabbi Halpern	Rabbi *or* Rabbi Halpern
Cantor	Cantor Richard Halpern	Dear Cantor Halpern	Cantor Halpern
Mormon			
Mormon Bishop	Bishop Robert Smith Church of the Latter Day Saints	Dear Mr. Smith	Bishop Churchill *or* Mr. Churchill
Protestant			
Clergyman Doctorate	The Reverend Doctor Thomas Churchill	Dear Dr. Churchill *or* Reverend Sir	Dr. Churchill
NonDoctorate	The Reverend Thomas Churchill	Dear Mr. Churchill *or* Reverend Sir	Mr. Churchill
Presiding Episcopal Bishop	The Most Reverend Thomas Churchill Presiding Bishop	Dear Bishop Churchill *or* Most Reverend Sir	Bishop Churchill
Episcopal Bishop	The Right Reverend Thomas Churchill Bishop of Washington	Dear Bishop Churchill *or* Right Reverend Sir	Bishop Churchill
Methodist Bishop	The Reverend Thomas Churchill Methodist Bishop of Washington	Dear Bishop Churchill *or* Reverend Sir	Bishop Churchill
Archdeacon	The Venerable Thomas Churchill Archdeacon of Washington	Dear Archdeacon Churchill *or* Venerable Sir	Archdeacon Churchill
Dean	The Very Reverend Thomas Churchill Dean of St. Paul's Cathedral	Dear Dean Churchill *or* Very Reverend Sir	Dean Churchill

GREETINGS & INTRODUCTIONS 35

PERSON	ADDRESS/INTRODUCTION	SALUTATION	CONVERSATION
Roman Catholic			
Pope	His Holiness, the Pope His Holiness, Pope John Paul II	Your Holiness *or* Most Holy Father	Your Holiness *or* Most Holy Father
Cardinal	His Eminence, James Cardinal Treacy	Dear Cardinal Treacy *or* Your Eminence	Cardinal Treacy *or* Your Eminence
Archbishop/ Bishop	Archbishop of Washington The Most Reverend James Treacy Archbishop/Bishop of Washington	Dear Arch./Bishop Treacy *or* Your Excellency	Archbishop/Bishop Treacy *or* Excellency
Monsignor	The Right Reverend Msgr. James Treacy	Dear Monsignor Treacy *or* Right Reverend Monsignor	Monsignor *or* Monsignor Treacy
Priest	The Reverend Father James Treacy	Dear Father Treacy *or* Reverend Father	Father *or* Father Treacy
Mother Superior	The Reverend Mother Mary Treacy	Dear Mother Treacy *or* Reverend Mother	Mother *or* Mother Treacy
Nun	Sister Mary Treacy	Dear Sister	Sister, Sister Mary *or* Sister Treacy
Brother	Brother James Treacy	Dear Brother James	Brother, Brother James *or* Brother Treacy

INVITATIONS & REPLIES

Invitational functions have become an integral part of business, ranging from a breakfast meeting to special occasion events. Such functions can be a welcome break from office routine, but they invariably carry a business overtone, even when the aim is strictly social. Therefore, while an executive (and his/her spouse) should look forward to such occasions, conservative behavior and observance of protocol is advised in these situations.

Most invitational functions today are considered to be semiformal or informal, and include such occasions as the business breakfast, lunch or dinner held in the executive dining room or at a restaurant; a luncheon or dinner honoring an individual or marking an event, held at a restaurant or hotel dining room/ballroom; a cocktail party or dinner held at an establishment or in the home of a business associate; and a picnic or similar type of function. Truly formal functions are relatively rare and are usually major corporate events.

Generally, invitations should be extended two to four weeks beforehand, depending on the type of function and when it is held. Invitations to large or important affairs, or to functions planned during a holiday season, should be sent at least three months in advance.

Types of Invitations

There are several accepted ways to extend an invitation:

- Telephone. Telephoned invitations are acceptable for most occasions, and are particularly appropriate when the function is in the nature of a business meeting (such as a business lunch), or when time and/or the number of invitees is limited. If a business social, specify whether spouses or guests are invited. If time permits, a follow-up reminder note or card, which specifies the particulars about the function, should be sent.
- Typewritten letter. Typewritten letters are appropriate for business-oriented functions or when the occasion requires a more detailed explanation.
- Mailgram. Mailgrams are an efficient method of invitation when time is of the essence.
- Fill-in engraved/printed card. Fill-in invitations are used for all types of functions. They contain standard wording, with blank spaces to write in the particulars about the function. Fill-in cards are available at stationers and widely used, because of their convenience and availability in an array of styles.
- Printed/thermographed card. Printed or thermographed (raised print) invitations are used for all types of functions. They may reflect the traditional style of an engraved invitation, or be creatively designed with different formatting, colors or in a way that reflects a company product or an aspect of the corporate image.
- Engraved card. Engraved invitations are reserved for the most formal and important of occasions. The traditional black lettering on white or ecru card stock is most common, but other color combinations may be utilized.

Content of Invitations

All invitations should contain complete information about the function. When the occasion calls for an engraved or printed invitation, the text is normally written in the "third person" style. Information is usually centered and, starting at the top, includes the following:

- Who is hosting the function. The organization's logo, followed by the name and title of the host executive(s) and/or organization name.
- A phrase such as "request(s) the pleasure of your company" or "cordially invite(s) you" follows next. When the invitation is also intended for one's spouse or guest, the phrase "requests the company of" or "requests the pleasure of the company of" (for example) "Dr. and Mrs. Edward Meyer" or "Ms. Katherine Bush and Guest" may appear on the invitation. [Alternatively, the envelope might be addressed to "Dr. and Mrs. Edward Meyer." The R.S.V.P. card may indicate that a guest is invited through provision of a line for the guest's name.]
- The type of function. The central activity of the occasion (e.g., "at a lecture and dinner" or "to a lecture and dinner") should be clearly stated.
- The purpose of the occasion. For instance, "to announce...," "commemorate," "honor," "introduce," "meet," "preview," or "recognize" is stated.
- When and at what time the function will occur. The day of the week and date (omitting the year) are given. If more than one activity is planned, the schedule should be specified here or in the lower right corner of the invitation (e.g., "Lecture from 7:00 to 8:00 P.M., Dinner at 8:00 P.M.").
- Where the function is to be held. Give the name and address of the site and, if applicable, the name of the banquet/meeting room.
- How to reply. R.S.V.P. is the abbreviation for *répondez s'il vous plaît*, meaning "please reply." The R.S.V.P. is located at the lower left corner of the invitation, giving the contact person's name and address and/or telephone number. R.S.V.P. is often omitted for larger cocktail parties (in such instances, one's spouse can be assumed to be invited as well). The R.S.V.P. may specify "Regrets Only," which simplifies responding. An

R.S.V.P. card and self-addressed return envelope may also be enclosed.
- The invitation should note additional information in the lower right corner, such as guidance about dress. Unless "Black Tie" or other dress requirement is stated, business attire is normally proper.
- A map should be provided with the invitation when those attending may be unfamiliar with the area where the function is being held or when directions are complicated.

An invitation might look like this:

COMPUPLAN

William A. McIntyre, President
of CompuPlan Corporation
requests the pleasure of the company of
Dr. and Mrs. Edward Meyer
at a dinner
to commemorate the firm's
Tenth Anniversary
on Saturday, September twenty-first
at eight o'clock
View Room
The Regency Hotel
Sunnyvale

R.S.V.P.
Ms. Elizabeth Hyde
3150 Tenth Street
Sunnyvale, CA 94086   *Cocktails*
(408) 555-1212   *at 7:00 P.M.*

A less traditionally styled invitation might appear as follows:

**CELLTECH
RESEARCH
COMPANY**

DAVID W. PATTERSON, CHAIRMAN
CORDIALLY INVITES YOU
TO THE PRESENTATION OF THE
TENTH ANNUAL KOHLBERG MEDAL
FOR DISTINGUISHED ACHIEVEMENT
IN BIOTECHNOLOGY RESEARCH

TO
DR. HELEN M. ERICKSON
LANGLEY RESEARCH UNIT
YALE UNIVERSITY

ON
SATURDAY, JULY 17TH
AT SEVEN O'CLOCK
THE GRAND BALLROOM
WALDORF-ASTORIA HOTEL
NEW YORK CITY

DINNER WILL BE SERVED
RSVP CARD ENCLOSED

Mailing Invitations

Invitations should be inserted into the envelope so that the text faces the back side of the envelope and the top coincides with the top of the envelope. Thus, when the card is taken out, the recipient can read the card without turning it over. Secondary materials, such as an R.S.V.P. card, are placed behind the invitation (or inside a double fold invitation) within the envelope. Envelope addresses should be typed or handwritten (do not use labels). Although the return address can be placed on the back flap, the Postal Service prefers the return address on the front, upper left corner of the envelope, to ensure its return if undeliverable.

Replies

Always respond promptly regarding your acceptance of an invitation, in accordance with instructions in the invitation or letter. Replies are made by telephone, handwritten or typewritten note, or R.S.V.P. card. For very formal occasions (absent a telephone number or response card), a formal written reply in the third person style is indicated. A formal reply for the first sample invitation above would be as follows:

> *Dr. and Mrs. Edward Meyer*
> *accept with pleasure*
> *the kind invitation of*
> *William A. McIntyre*
> *President of CompuPlan Corporation*
> *for dinner*
> *on Saturday, September twenty-first.*

Other Responsibilities

Cancelling an Acceptance.
There are few acceptable reasons for not showing or cancelling after you have accepted an invitation. A cancellation of your initial acceptance should be briefly explained, with a sincere apology. Cancellations should be telephoned as soon as possible and, for very important functions, followed with a written note.

Bringing a Guest.
As a single person, you should not request to bring a guest to a seated meal in a colleague's home—the host should indicate to you if a guest is welcome. At some functions, such as a large buffet or cocktail party, it may be acceptable to bring a guest, but you should first ask the host.

Reciprocating an Invitation.
Generally, those who attend business functions need not reciprocate with an invitation. Invitations to social functions, however, should be reciprocated. Although the return invitation need not be in kind, it should be at the same "level." For example, if you and your spouse were invited to an elaborate dinner at the home of a colleague, you could reciprocate with an invitation to join you for dinner at a better restaurant or a stage production.

Inviting a Superior.
Junior executives should be cautious about inviting a superior (and spouse) to a restaurant or his home for dinner. This would be appropriate only if the junior executive and his spouse had already been to the superior's home for dinner or they had known the superior and his spouse for a long period of time.

Thank Yous.
Upon departing a business/social function, comment favorably on the occasion and offer a sincere expression of thanks to the host. Following the function, a verbal thank you at the office or a thank you note sent to the host, although not required, are thoughtful gestures. A written note should particularly be considered when the function is primarily social and is held at the home of a colleague.

Presentations/Speaking

Most businesspersons are called upon to make prepared presentations as a requirement of their position. As the speaker, you need to optimize your preparation, delivery and stage presence in order to effectively present a message. This not only helps in promoting your ideas, but fulfills the responsibility you have to provide credible information to those in attendance. Because public speaking conveys an "image" about the speaker *and* the firm he/she represents, speaking ability can play a prominent role in one's advancement within the organization. It is therefore worth the effort to work on improving your speaking skills.

Preparation

It is very important that you thoroughly prepare before any presentation.

- Your presentation should be well organized by having a clear introduction and purpose or thesis, a body that focuses on the salient points you want to make, and an ending that provides a summary of the main points and conclusions.
- The text should be logically and concisely constructed. Utilize concrete examples and statistical data to illustrate and support your statements. Avoid rambling thoughts and statements.
- The language you use should be kept relatively simple, and terminology should be readily understandable to the

audience.
- Think ahead about questions that might be asked and how you will respond.
- Practice your presentation in front of a mirror or, preferably, audiotape or videotape record your presentation. Listen carefully for voice characteristics; you will want to articulate words with good diction and an agreeable pitch, tonal quality, tempo or rate of speech, and volume of sound. Observe body movements—notice your posture, facial expressiveness, and arm and hand gestures. Work on problem areas and re-record yourself to determine if improvements are evident. If possible, conduct a "dry run" in the presence of a colleague.
- If you are using slides or other visual aids, incorporate them into your practice session. Make sure the visuals are properly sequenced and correspond with what you are saying, that they truly add substance to the presentation, are professional in appearance, and are large enough to be read at the back of the meeting room.
- Ensure that you finish the presentation within set time constraints.
- If not already known, familiarize yourself with the background and expectations of the audience so that, with this knowledge, you are more comfortable when speaking before them.
- Visit the meeting room beforehand to familiarize yourself with the setting, and to check on the working order and use of audiovisual equipment.
- Finally, use mental imagery to visualize yourself making the presentation, effectively and with confidence. Visualize this as a positive experience.

Delivery

The style of delivery may vary with the type of meeting. However, certain general statements can be made.

PRESENTATIONS/SPEAKING **45**

- Take a slow, deep breath and mentally calm yourself. Begin by thanking the person who introduced you and, if appropriate, by greeting distinguished guests and then the audience.
- Establish rapport with the audience. For instance, open with remarks or a humorous anecdote that relates yourself or the subject of the presentation with the audience or the meeting location.
- Use proper grammar and a good working vocabulary that is natural and suited to your style. Avoid the following: hesitations; filler words/phrases such as "uh" or "you know;" slang or words that are of passing fashion; and lingo or technical jargon (unless appropriate for the audience).
- Unless giving a formal speech, it is usually best to use cards or papers on which key thoughts and phrases are written in outline form, rather than utilize a complete manuscript. Highlighting the outline or using margin notes can be helpful in identifying places in the presentation where more verbal emphasis is indicated.
- Visually, you should slowly pan over the audience, breaking regularly to make eye contact with individual members of the audience.
- Your voice should be well modulated. Avoid being monotonal. Appropriate variations in pitch, tempo and volume of your voice make your thoughts more convincing and interesting to listen to.
- When using visual aids, use a pointer to indicate specific items on the visual that correspond with the content of your presentation, and speak to the audience (not toward the visual) whenever possible.
- If you take audience questions in a large room without the benefit of floor microphones, you should first repeat the question so that everyone may hear it.
- End the presentation on a "solid" or uplifting note.

Stage Presence

- Aside from greater visibility, standing and/or using a podium will impart more authority, control and formality to the meeting.
- Good body language is particularly important. Confidence and poise are conveyed by projecting a calm and friendly facial disposition, and maintaining an erect, but relaxed posture. Gesturing of the arms and hands is very effective if it is natural, sincere and not overdone. Avoid nervous mannerisms such as fidgeting with your hands.
- Always have a handkerchief available to use when you are about to cough or sneeze; simply cover your mouth with it and turn your head away from the audience and microphone. Avoid having pocket coins or jewelry that might jingle when you move.
- An authoritative personal appearance is important. You should always be well groomed and, unless presenting at a resort location, dressed in conservative business attire that is in current style.

Introducing the Speaker

The introduction of a speaker should be brief and upbeat. As the introducer, you should acquaint the audience with the speaker, mentioning significant aspects of his background and accomplishments (personalize this information when possible). Relate the reason for, or content of the presentation to the audience and pique their interest in what the speaker is about to say.

Immediately following the address, you should thank the speaker and comment on the excellence (or informative nature, etc.) of the presentation. If this also concludes the meeting program, thank the audience for their attendance at the function.

TELECOMMUNICATION

Telephone manners have a decided impact on the perception others have about one's business or profession. Telephone calls that are handled intelligently, in a pleasant, helpful and professional manner, say that you care about the caller and have character as a business entity. Secretarial and other office staff who answer telephones should therefore be well trained. For the increasing number of executives who answer their own telephone and place outgoing calls directly, proper telephone skills are also very important.

Answering the Telephone

- Answer the telephone promptly, preferably not later than the third ring, with a pleasant voice.
- Greet the caller with the business name ("Platten Architects"), or the division or executive's name if the business name is felt nonessential (e.g., "Project Management" or "Mr. Wiley's office").
- An additional statement may be made such as "Good morning" (before or after the business name), "Ms. Davis speaking," or "May I help you."
- If answering your own telephone (on a direct inward dialing system), do not answer with a simple "Hello." Greet the caller with your name only if the organizational name is felt nonessential (e.g., "Mr. Wiley," "Mr. Wiley speaking," or "Hello, this is Mr. Wiley"). The business or division name may also be used before or after your own name (e.g., "Mr. Wiley, Project Management").

- When using a given name or nickname, do so only in conjunction with the surname (e.g., "Jonathan Wiley's office;" "Jon Wiley speaking").
- If the caller fails to identify him/herself, say "May I ask who is calling, please?"
- After the telephone caller has identified himself, the telephone call may be screened. Questions such as "What company are you with, please?" and/or, "Would Mr. Wiley know what this is in reference to?" or "May I ask what this is in reference to?" are appropriate. Call screening is an accepted business practice that, for certain organizations, expedites the handling of telephone calls. However, for many other businesses, the practice should be restricted due to its perception by the caller as being somewhat intrusive. Because tact is required, only a skilled and knowledgeable secretary should perform this function.
- Place a caller on hold for no more than 30 to 40 seconds. If the caller is on hold much longer, apologize for the delay. If the caller is willing to remain on hold for an extended period while waiting for information or for someone to come on the line, periodically check back with the caller until the information is ready or the connection is made.
- When the person requested is not available, state the reason for his unavailability (do not respond with an ambiguous statement such as "He is not in," but do use judgment) and ask if you may (1) help the caller or refer the caller to someone else; (2) take a message; and/or (3) take the caller's name and telephone number and have the person return the call. When taking a caller's name, telephone number and message, utilize printed telephone message pads and record all required information. Repeat a lengthy message to the caller in order to ensure that it has been accurately recorded.
- If the telephone call is to be transferred, provide the caller with an explanation, plus the name and telephone

number of the party to whom the caller is being forwarded. This provides the caller with useful information as well as the new telephone number in the event of a disconnection.
- Always be courteous, even to a disagreeable caller.

Placing a Telephone Call

- Prepare before making the telephone call, and have available any written materials which pertain to the subject of the call.
- Do place your own telephone calls whenever possible. Always place the call yourself to a more senior executive, rather than through your secretary.
- If you dial the wrong number, apologize.
- Identify yourself when requesting to speak with the other party (e.g., "This is Jon Wiley calling. Is Sharon Lewis in?").
- Do not be annoyed if asked by a secretary about your affiliation or the nature of your call. Offer the information or, if applicable, state that you are returning a call or that it is a personal matter.
- If the person you are calling is unavailable and you plan on being out of your office during a specific time period, indicate to the person recording the information when it is best to return the call.

Telephone Conversation

- Before conversing on the telephone, lower any background noise that could be audible.
- Discuss the business matter with direction so as to not waste the other person's time; this is especially important during a multiperson conference call.
- Show interest in the other person's conversation by an occasional "Yes," "I know," or other such comment,

and take notes to which you can then refer for subsequent questions or statements.
- If you must converse with someone who is present in your office, excuse yourself, place the telephone party on hold, and quickly complete whatever is pressing and return to the telephone call.
- Finish the business discussion on an affirmative note that indicates you have had a useful and/or pleasant conversation.

Additional Guidelines

- Return calls promptly, and within the same day.
- Do not receive telephone calls during a preset appointment with someone in your office. If you must answer the telephone, tell the caller that you are in a meeting and will return the call as soon as possible.
- If the telephone call is disconnected, it is the responsibility of the person who initiated the call to call back immediately, regardless of cause of the disconnection.
- If you are going to an office to meet with someone who is on the telephone, do not enter his office unless you are motioned in. Similarly, if you are in the office of a colleague who takes a call, offer to leave the office; if the conversation is personal, quietly exit while gesturing that you will wait outside the office.
- The acceptability of making business-related telephone calls to staff persons at home will vary. Many companies believe that business calls to the home of managers or principals in the firm goes with their position. Regardless, some acknowledgment of the possible inconvenience of the call should be made before starting the conversation.

You should not undervalue the importance of telephone etiquette. Take the time to ensure that all staff are familiar with good telephone techniques.

2 · MEETINGS/CONFERENCES

THE CHAIRPERSON

THE PARTICIPANTS

OFFICE APPOINTMENTS

OFFSITE APPOINTMENTS

JOB INTERVIEWS

BOARD OF DIRECTORS MEETINGS

CONFERENCES

Meetings are endemic in business—they take many forms and are called for various purposes. Meetings serve the needs of the organization and are a forum for participants. The effectiveness of a meeting relates directly to the meeting skills of the chairperson and those in attendance. This Chapter provides guidance on optimizing one's personal effectiveness in business meetings.

Meetings/Conferences

Effective meetings are essential to proper management of a business. Meetings are called for the purposes of planning activities, providing information, solving problems and making decisions. Types of business meetings include the impromptu meeting in a colleague's office, appointments with others (interoffice personnel, clients, consultants, salespersons), regular policy or staff meetings, interdepartmental meetings, senior executive meetings, board of directors meetings and conferences.

While the person who conducts a meeting is usually the most visible, each person at the meeting is on view. As a participant, you are compared to, and evaluated by those in attendance on the basis of your mannerisms, how you think, and generally how you handle yourself and interact with others—in other words, you are judged on the basis of personal qualities and professional competence. Meetings are therefore important in not only furthering the work of the organization, but can be a determinant in whether you advance and achieve your potential within the organization.

The Meeting Chairperson

The individual who leads a meeting sets the direction and tone of the proceedings, and has the responsibility to exercise control in a way that fosters and maintains productive communication among the participants. The degree of control will depend on the meeting agenda and attendees. For the uninitiated, this can be a challenge when controversial

54 EXECUTIVE ETIQUETTE

issues are before the group. It is therefore important that the chairperson be capable and knowledgeable, and someone in whom the participants have confidence. There are certain things to keep in mind when chairing a meeting.

Pre-Meeting.
- The reason for calling the meeting and the objectives to be met should be clear. Select the persons to be invited as meeting participants accordingly.
- Schedule the meeting at a convenient date, time and location, and establish an ending time.
- When the type of meeting or number of discussion items calls for it, prepare an agenda with the topics prioritized, such that the more important items will be considered first. Research all issues, as necessary, and send the agenda and any background information to participants in advance of the meeting. For meetings such as staff meetings, provide the participants an opportunity to suggest items for the agenda before it is finalized.
- The size of the meeting room should be consistent with the number of participants. Ensure that the room is clean, comfortable, well ventilated and generally conducive to the conduct of a productive meeting. All audiovisual equipment should be set up in advance of the meeting.
- Designate a secretary or meeting participant to prepare notes of the meeting.

During the Meeting.
- Begin the meeting on time, particularly for regularly scheduled meetings. For special meetings or those held with attendees from outside the firm, delay the starting time a few minutes if it is evident that some participants are not yet present.
- Introduce participants, as appropriate. State the purpose and objectives of the meeting. Announce the scheduled ending time of the meeting.

- Facilitate and encourage open discussion of the issues. Show interest in the discussions by posing questions and highlighting significant points. Tactfully deter those who begin to dominate the proceedings, and call on other persons who might have knowledge of the subject. Show patience and impartiality in dealing with all participants.
- Keep participants "on track" with the agenda, in terms of the topics, objectives and time of the meeting. Providing a brief progress summary during a lengthy discussion is sometimes helpful. If it appears that insufficient time has been allotted to cover all agenda items, discuss possible options (e.g., items that should be discussed, referred to a committee, or could be postponed until a later meeting) with the participants before continuing on with the meeting.
- At the conclusion of the meeting, summarize the discussions and results. Recap follow-up actions to be taken, the persons responsible for specified tasks and time frame for their completion. Thank the participants for their attendance and contributions to the meeting.
- End the meeting on time (occasionally, the subject under discussion may warrant a continuance).
- If notes of the proceedings are made, distribute meeting minutes or a summary of meeting highlights within a few days to all participants, including those who were unable to be present.

Meeting Notes.
It is good business practice to prepare either meeting minutes or a summary of meeting highlights in order to document discussions and any decisions agreed to. A meeting record is particularly important when complex, controversial or critical issues are deliberated. By providing an archival record of the proceedings, meeting notes enhance communication and promote accountability within the organization.

The chairperson should designate one person in advance of the meeting to take notes. If the use of a tape recorder is contemplated, obtain the consent of meeting participants beforehand. The chairperson and participants should also plan to write down important points during the meeting, which can be compared with the official minutes to ensure there are no discrepancies that could lead to misunderstanding.

Businesses will often establish a format or use a standard form for the written record. Following are some general guidelines on preparing meeting notes.

- Notes should accurately and concisely capture the essence of discussions; they should objectively report the issues covered and be devoid of characterizations. A verbatim account is ordinarily required only for decisions, actions, motions and resolutions (also include the originator).
- Standard elements may include the name or type of meeting; location, date and time; name of the chairperson/presiding officer; names (and affiliation, if needed) of persons in attendance and absent; purpose or subject; the order of business; time of adjournment; and, names and signatures of the recording person and chairperson.
- Notes should be logically organized. Notes might correspond with the agenda or order of business; follow an outline in which topics are grouped into categories; or be rearranged so that conclusions, decisions and actions are given first, followed by the pertinent background discussions.
- The meeting minutes should be reviewed by the chairperson prior to finalization.
- Usually, minutes are distributed as soon as possible to all participants, who should review them for accuracy. Corrections should be brought to the attention of the chairperson or noted at the next convening of the meeting, as appropriate.

The Meeting Participants

Participants also have certain responsibilities which help produce a more effective meeting.

Pre-Meeting.
- Be thoroughly prepared. Know the purpose of the meeting. If available, review the agenda, and obtain and read background materials prior to the meeting. If issues suggest possible conflict, learn who else will be at the meeting and try to resolve identifiable problems with colleagues before the meeting is held.
- When making a presentation, conduct a "dry run," preferably in the presence of a trusted colleague who will provide you with a candid assessment. Experts agree that it is better to write down and present from key thoughts, rather than read from a complete manuscript (unless, of course, you are giving a formal speech). Ensure that any slides or other visual aids add substance to the presentation, are professional in appearance, and can be read at the back of the conference room. (See also the Section entitled "Presentations/Speaking").

During the Meeting.
- Be on time—it is distracting to enter the office or conference room and be seated when the meeting is in progress.
- If you are a newcomer to a regularly held meeting, allow others to take their seats before seating yourself. As a sign of respect for a professional colleague (and not the end of chivalrous courtesy), men need not rise when a woman executive enters the meeting room, nor need they assist with her chair. Be cognizant about the organizational significance placed on who sits in the "power" or authority positions at a conference table (e.g., the head of the table, the immediate right and left of the head position, center chairs).

- Be attentive and speak-up, but do not dominate a discussion. The effectiveness of a meeting is realized only when the participants maintain interest and active involvement in the discussions—stay alert and express your viewpoints. If you are bored, avoid displaying poor habits such as whispering to your neighbor, slouching in your chair, repetitious checking of your watch, or doodling. Although some persons may be hesitant to ask for clarification or to express their opinions, most fears are unfounded and, in fact, even seemingly simple questions often contribute to the understanding of other meeting participants. On the other hand, think before you speak. It is unwise to speak at length on a subject about which you know little or nothing; or, as an authority on the subject, to take over a conversation to the exclusion of others.
- Stay with the focus of the meeting. Everyone's time is valuable, no matter what their position in the organization. Many tangential (and some not so tangential) issues may be brought up in the course of a meeting. Unless there is concurrence that the new subject be discussed, it is better to postpone further deliberation on the matter.
- Be considerate of the thoughts and feelings of others. Meeting participants should feel free to offer ideas, ask questions and discuss issues openly. Because people often perceive matters differently or are not versed in the nuances of all subject matters, any derision of others is out of place in a meeting. Do not personalize negative remarks; rather, phrase critical comments in such a way that they will be received in the constructive sense that is intended. When on the receiving end of an unduly negative comment, do not respond in kind; keep reactive emotions under control.
- Inform the chairperson beforehand if it is likely that you will have to leave during the meeting.

Office Appointments

Business meetings held in your office afford the opportunity to discuss a matter in detail, but the effectiveness of such meetings can be short-circuited if a few courtesies are overlooked. This is particularly true when the appointment is with visitors from outside your organization. Therefore, in addition to principles already given, be alert to the following.

- Be on schedule. Do not let prior meetings overrun their scheduled allotment of time. If you must keep colleagues or visitors waiting, you or your secretary should inform them of the approximate time delay and ensure their comfort.
- When other than your co-workers, you should stand and welcome all meeting attendees (e.g., visitors, senior company officials), offering a handshake in greeting to both men and women. Introduce the meeting participants to each other and gesture to be seated (ensure that there are enough chairs before the participants arrive). A few pleasantries help to relax participants, and beverages should be offered, if appropriate. Normally, you need only wear your jacket when meeting with senior management and visitors from outside the firm.
- Once the meeting has begun, do not receive telephone calls. If a call must be taken, inform the caller that you are in a meeting, and either conduct the business quickly or offer to return the call as soon as the meeting is finished.
- Listen attentively, ask questions and take notes. If the visitor is there to promote an idea or market a product, allow the person adequate time to discuss the matter; always be polite.
- At the conclusion of the meeting, summarize the proceedings. Comment about the usefulness of the meeting, thank the visitor(s) and exchange handshakes, and escort him/her to the door.

Offsite Appointments

Business appointments at the office of outside executives also involve certain courtesies.

- Prepare well and collect any written materials you will need to take with you.
- Dress conservatively and ensure a neat appearance.
- Be on time. If you expect to arrive late, telephone ahead and inform the person you are to meet.
- If you must wait before being shown into the person's office, do so patiently.
- Introduce yourself to the other executive(s) if you have not previously met. Allow the host executive or person whose office you are in direct you to a chair, rather than taking any available seat.
- Allow the presiding person to open the meeting.
- If you are making a presentation, begin by stating the purpose of the visit; then, avoid being verbose.
- Show interest in the executive's comments. Listen carefully, ask questions, and take notes.
- Unless there is some reason to the contrary, try not to put the person you are visiting on the spot by requesting immediate decisions.
- Keep in mind the time allotted for the meeting and stay within the set limit.
- Summarize pertinent information at the conclusion of the meeting, and thank the host executive.

Job Interviews

Job interviews are situations in which all participants want to be particularly well mannered. The interviewer wants the applicant to carry away a favorable impression of the firm, and the applicant wants to show that he can fit into the organization with ease. Some general guidelines are recommended for the conduct of an interview.

Interviewer.
- As the interviewer, you should be knowledgeable about proper interviewing techniques and have good listening skills.
- Review the firm's written job/position description. Read the person's application, résumé and any letters of recommendation beforehand.
- Write questions that you will want to ask the applicant, and be mindful of significant points about the position and firm which you want to convey.
- Be aware of any biases you might have, so as to avoid them during the interview.
- When the applicant arrives, stand and greet him with a firm handshake and offer a place to be seated.
- Set a relaxed tone at the outset of the meeting. Open with a warm welcome and a few pleasantries.
- Be attentive; ask properly phrased questions to elicit the information you need to make an objective evaluation; and listen carefully to the applicant's responses and questions. Be aware of any nonverbal communication.
- Keep the interview directed, but nonrushed.
- Bring the interview to a close by summarizing the discussion, asking if there are any more questions and informing the applicant when he can expect to hear about a decision. Thank the applicant for coming, shake hands and escort him to the door.

Interviewee.
- As the interviewee, you should prepare well in advance of the interview. Learn as much as possible about the firm and the position for which you are applying. Think of questions about the position you will want to ask, and the attributes about yourself which you want to emphasize. Additionally, consider those questions that may be asked of you and how you will respond to them.
- Bring any written materials you may need, such as samples of your work, selected letters of commendation

and copies of your résumé.
- Proper appearance is essential. Clothing should be appropriate for the position—this will normally be conservative business attire that is meticulously clean, pressed, and in style. Ensure also that you present a neat and well groomed appearance.
- Be on time for the interview. Arriving a bit early may help accustom you to the surroundings.
- Be attentive; listen carefully to the interviewer's questions, and ask for clarification if you do not understand something.
- Give complete and honest responses. Do not answer with a simple "yes" or "no" when a more detailed response is indicated, and do not ramble on.
- Maintain good eye contact with the interviewer.
- At the conclusion of the interview, thank the interviewer and shake hands.
- A written thank you note, that includes a reiteration of a few significant points and your continued interest in the position, might also be sent to the interviewer, but this should be done within a day or two of the interview.

Résumé.

Résumés are used in making determinations about a person's fitness for a position, and they are often utilized to screen prospective candidates even before job interviews and reference checks are considered. Résumés are also needed for inclusion in contract proposals, and as background material for the development of award nominations and the introduction of speakers, among other things. Because of their importance, the content of a résumé should be very carefully thought out in advance. The following are some general guidelines for preparing a résumé.

- Plan to limit the length of the résumé to no more than two typewritten pages.
- The first part of the résumé provides identifier data,

including your full name, home or office address and telephone number. Optionally, personal data such as birth date and place, marital status and number of children are placed here or at the end.
- Second (optionally), a paragraph which succinctly describes your most significant accomplishments and career objectives is given.
- Third, professional qualifications are provided (education or work experience may precede):
  - Education—for each college or university attended, the name, years of attendance (optional), certificates/degrees and year awarded.
  - Work experience—for each job held, the employment dates, company affiliation, position title, and a brief statement of responsibilities and notable achievements.
  - Other relevant activities—business or professional memberships, community service, consultantships, honors, publications, et cetera.

  Information under education and work experience is normally presented in inverse chronologic order, beginning with the most recent data. You should accentuate your "strong points," but do not misrepresent factual information through overstatement. Always be completely truthful.
- Fourth, a statement such as "References available upon request" is placed at the end of the résumé. You should have ready a list of those persons who have agreed to serve as references.
- Finally, date the résumé with the month and year.
- It is vital that the résumé be well written. Write clearly and concisely, use proper syntax, and ensure that you use and spell all words properly.
- The résumé should have a balanced appearance on the page. Typing must be flawless. Use text embellishers such as character bolding or underlining to improve readability.
- Only originals, printed copies or photocopies with excel-

64 EXECUTIVE ETIQUETTE

lent reproduction should be used.
- It is important to customize the résumé for each type of position for which you are applying.

A thoughtfully written cover letter should accompany the résumé when it is sent to prospective employers. The letter should indicate the reason for your interest in the position and firm. It should highlight your attributes and pique the interest of the recipient to peruse the résumé. Keep the letter relatively brief, and be certain that it has a professional appearance.

Board of Directors Meetings

When a board of directors is present, it serves an essential role in the operations of the organization. Because of its importance, the board must be fully informed about all pertinent matters. Management has the responsibility to keep the board apprised of developments, and should be responsive to the needs of the board. Company officials and board members should always be mindful of the impact of their interactions with one another.

A "Board Book" containing an agenda, minutes of the previous meeting and information pertaining to each reporting area should be sent to board members in advance of all meetings. In preparation for the meeting, a folder containing paper, pencil or pen and documents relevant to the day's proceedings is placed at each member's position at the conference table.

Aside from the principles noted earlier in this Section, the chairperson will normally follow an established order of business that includes the following: calling the meeting to order; reading the minutes of the last meeting; presenting officer and committee reports; discussing unfinished business; introducing new business for discussion; presentation of programs, if any; and adjournment. Board of directors meetings are usually conducted with some formality, and the reference, *Robert's Rules of Order*, should be in use.

Conferences

While the terms "meeting" and "conference" can be used interchangeably, conferences generally tend to be larger and more structured, and involve a series of presentations. Conferences, seminars, business conventions and other large meetings are often held away from the office, and require significant planning by the sponsor. Because conference centers and hotels with such facilities may be reserved months or even years in advance, such meetings must be scheduled early on. Some firms have a trained conference planner(s) on their staff who can make the necessary site, transportation and publicity arrangements, and there are also consultant services which specialize in conference planning.

As with all meetings, the conference purpose should be clear. A planning committee should be constituted to develop the program and list of invited speakers. Candidate speakers may initially be contacted by telephone to learn of their interest, following which a confirmation letter is sent, as applicable. Speakers should be given specific information about program objectives and time requirements. It is advisable for the sponsoring firm to request abstracts of the presentations at an early date, to ensure that objectives will be attained.

Considerations such as program schedule, estimated attendance, size of rooms needed for presentations, equipment needs, and any refreshment service requirements must be discussed with the conference planner.

Needless to say, conference attendees should follow basic rules of decorum. In addition to the business sessions, conference sponsors often provide social functions at which colleagues and associates can meet and interact. In whatever setting, be aware of your behavior and how it will impact on your reputation.

3 • DINING/ENTERTAINING

COCKTAIL FUNCTIONS

RESTAURANT DINING MANNERS

TABLE MANNERS

TABLE SETTINGS

Dining and entertaining are a part of business life. It is generally held that one's dining skills reflect upbringing, but in business, ability at the dining table also influences the perception of others with respect to a person's professional competence. Businesspersons need, therefore, to be adept in this area. This Chapter provides guidance in proper dining etiquette.

COCKTAIL FUNCTIONS

Cocktail parties offer a means to renew professional relationships, and to meet and socialize with many people at one place and time. Occasions where cocktails are served as a primary part of the function include the cocktail party, cocktail-buffet party, the predinner cocktail hour, and receptions. The societal trend toward a reduction in the consumption of alcohol simply means that there should be a wider selection of nonalcoholic beverages available at the function for guests. In all cases, there are some general considerations which should be kept in mind.

Considerations for the Host

Plan Well.
There are many items to consider when planning a cocktail function.

- Telephone or send written invitations at least two to three weeks in advance of a party. The beginning *and* ending time of the function should be specified. For the sake of efficiency, the R.S.V.P. on written invitations may state "Regrets Only" with a telephone number.
- The room for the function should be large enough for guests to easily wander about without jostling each other. The room must be well ventilated.
- Ensure a reasonably well stocked liquor selection. If the function is held in the home, liquor should include gin, vodka, bourbon, scotch, sherry and vermouth, along with white wine, beer, mixers, soda, tonic and mineral water, and a variety of low calorie and nonalcoholic bev-

erages. Ice and garnishes should be in plentiful supply. In estimating the number of bottles of liquor that will be needed, plan on three drinks for every guest present. A liter or quart bottle of liquor will yield 21 drinks (using a 1 1/2 ounce jigger), which will therefore serve about seven guests.

- At a cocktail function in the home, ensure a sufficient quantity of the following: glasses (including, at a minimum, highball, on-the-rocks, and all purpose wine glasses); cocktail napkins; coasters; toothpicks; ash trays; and, a few strategically placed bar trays for used glasses and napkins.
- At a cocktail party, munchy finger food should be distributed around the room. If hors d'oeuvres are served, a good variety and amount of quality cold and hot foods should be provided.
- Locate bars in accessible areas and have enough of them so that drink lines will remain short.
- Bartenders, waiters and waitresses should be given specific instructions. They should be neatly groomed and appropriately attired.
- At larger functions, company staff should be available to facilitate guest introductions, conviviality, and to assist with the beverage and food service.

Time and Length of Function.

Business cocktail functions are usually scheduled between the hours of 5:00 p.m. and 8:00 p.m., with cocktail-buffets scheduled between 6:00 p.m. and 10:00 p.m. Dinner schedules are variable. The starting time of these functions is often somewhat later on workdays than on weekends. Two hours are normally allowed for cocktail parties and receptions, with the bar closed 15 to 30 minutes after the scheduled ending time. Cocktail-buffets usually last two or three hours. The duration of dinners is variable; for the social hour at a dinner, limit predinner drinks to 45 minutes or an hour.

COCKTAIL FUNCTIONS

Greeting Guests.
Unless the function is a large, convention-type reception, guests should be greeted upon arrival and helped with any coats, hats and umbrellas. They should be briefed on the layout of bars and food tables, and introduced to other guests who are present.

Handling Difficult Guests.
Unwelcome hangers-on and guests who are inebriated should be dealt with firmly, but with tact and kindness. The host is normally responsible for the safety of guests, and anyone who appears functionally impaired must be assisted in whatever way necessary to ensure that the person is safely returned to his/her home or hotel. If necessary, overnight accommodations should be arranged for the person.

Considerations for the Guest

Be on Time.
It is important to be on time. For cocktail parties and receptions, arrival should be no later than 15 to 30 minutes after the starting time. Normally, for pre-dinner drinks, cocktail-buffets and primarily business functions, one should arrive within 15 minutes of the scheduled starting time.

Badges.
At large receptions, guests may be given name badges. Badges should be placed on the right coat lapel or area of clothing which covers the right upper chest—in this position, people can most easily glance at one another's badge when they meet and shake hands.

Consuming Beverages.
Always use a cocktail napkin with iced drinks to con-

tain dripping and to avoid presenting a cold, wet hand in a handshake. Most importantly, consume alcoholic drinks conservatively. It is very difficult to regain a reputation for stability and being in control when your conversation or behavior has publicly deteriorated due to alcohol intake. Tips include the following: decide beforehand on a specific limit to the number of alcoholic drinks you order; sip the drinks slowly; and, alternate with nonalcoholic drinks if the function is particularly long. Do not linger around the immediate bar area after receiving your drink.

Consuming Food.
Whatever the type of function, do not overindulge. Avoid standing near the hors d'oeuvres or buffet table for long periods of time, so you do not give the appearance of being wedded to the food and to allow easy access to the table by other guests.

Conversation.
Topics of discussion at a cocktail function should generally be light. Unless a business function, office matters should be avoided, especially in the presence of a senior executive, unless that person initiates the subject. Give full attention to the person with whom you are talking; avoid the "glazed" eye look or allowing your eyes to wander. Do not "unload" particularly personal information which could make you or the listener uneasy when back in the office.

Follow-up.
If, after accepting an invitation to a function, you are unable to attend, you should telephone the host as soon as possible. If you are unexpectedly unable to attend at the time of the function, contact the host immediately (if appropriate) or the next day with an apology and a brief explanation for your absence. After attending a function (particularly when hosted by a colleague), it is a good idea to send a thank you note.

Restaurant Dining Manners

Business entertaining in a restaurant may be for the purpose of conducting business, marking a business occasion, or may be primarily social in nature. Whatever the purpose, restaurant dining requires a familiarity with proper procedures and manners, in addition to general table etiquette (see the Sections entitled "Table Manners" and "Table Settings"). It is a fact that executives win and lose business accounts and promotions, simply on the basis of the manners they display at the restaurant dining table.

Reservations

If you are the host of a business lunch or dinner, you will be responsible for all arrangements and coordination of the meal. Planning ahead, particularly for larger groups, is often essential to ensure a successful event. The restaurant should be chosen based on the desired ambience for the function, preferences (if known) of the guests, and convenience of location. When telephoning the restaurant to make the reservation, you should specify any special requirements or service you want, such as requesting a nonsmoking or more secluded area of the restaurant, or requesting a certain method for paying the bill.

For very important occasions, visit the restaurant beforehand and confirm all arrangements, including, if applicable, where individuals are to sit. You should also consider providing the maître d' (headwaiter) with a substantive tip in advance of the function.

Arrival and Seating

The host should be at the restaurant early enough to greet arriving guests. Upon arrival, guests should check overcoats and umbrellas at the checkroom. If you know that you will be more than a few minutes late, telephone the restaurant. If the host or some of the guests have not arrived on time, the maître d' should be so informed by those present. They usually then have the option of staying at the restaurant's waiting area or proceeding to the table to wait for the others to arrive. The maître d' will lead your party to the dining table; in a small group, women and then men should follow the maître d' to the table.

Nothing on the dining table should be disturbed while waiting for others. If, however, ten to fifteen minutes have elapsed and everyone is still not present, begin with the drink orders. It is generally recommended that a person limit oneself to one or at most two cocktails or glasses of wine before the meal. "Nondrinkers" (especially the host, if a nondrinker) should consider ordering a nonalcoholic beverage. If someone you know is seated elsewhere in the restaurant, avoid leaving the table, but merely nod in acknowledgement to the other person if eye contact is made.

As guests arrive at the table, the host should greet and introduce them, as appropriate, and indicate where they are to be seated. The best seats, such as armchairs, seats which are away from busy aisles or the banquette (the bench seat along the wall), should be given to clients or guests. If you need the undivided attention of a person(s) to discuss business matters, consider requesting a table in a secluded part of the restaurant. Men and women should be dispersed around the table, such that there is no apparent segregation. At larger functions where there is an honored guest, he/she is seated to the right of the host.

Ordering

Food.
The host should recommend a few items on the menu for which the restaurant is noted and suggest, if budget is not a concern, one or two expensive main courses to signal to guests that they should feel free to order what they want. Otherwise, guests should select a moderately priced menu item (in other words, select neither the least or most expensive item, because either might be a slight to the host). Items are ordered à la carte, where each item is separately priced, or table d'hôte, a complete meal for a set price. Guests should not hesitate to ask the captain of the table or waiter about specialty dishes or for his recommendation. On the other hand, it is unwise at business lunches or dinners to ask the waiter about a dish you should ordinarily know about (refer to the "Glossary of Foods" on page 78) or when you are unsure how to pronounce it. When the primary function of the meal is to conduct business, ease of consumption should also be kept in mind when selecting the main course. Each person should order for himself, and be ready to answer the waiter's inquiries about selections and food preparation.

Wine.
After all food orders are taken, the host should order wine, if it is desired. The wine order will be taken by the waiter or a wine steward (sommelier). The host who has little knowledge of wines should either ask the waiter/wine steward for his recommendation or ask a knowledgeable guest to make the selection. A good quality wine should be chosen, based on what most people have selected for their main course. White and red wines may both be ordered, although a carefully chosen white or red wine will often complement any combination of foods. (See "Wine Service" on page 83 for additional information.)

Conversation

If the function is a business meal, the host should initiate the business discussion. Conversation should be limited to small talk until the waiter has taken everyone's order, including the wine order, and removed the menus; only then should business discussions commence. If the function is more social in nature, each guest has some responsibility to ensure that his neighbors at the table are included in conversation. For example, after conversing for a while with the person to his right, a diner should turn to the neighbor on his left and initiate a dialogue.

Eating

Eating should begin only after everyone has been served, unless it is apparent that the service is unduly delayed and to wait would result in the meals already served becoming cold. If there is a guest of honor, he should begin eating first, followed by the other guests and then the host. Absent an honored guest, the host should urge everyone to begin if there is hesitation.

In addition to the information contained in the Sections "Table Manners" and "Table Settings," there are several things to note when eating in a restaurant:

- It is the host's responsibility to manage the table and call a waiter to the table when needed. Guests should keep complaints to a minimum and quietly convey any problems to the host or, at larger affairs or absent a host, to the waiter.
- If an uncut loaf of bread is served, the host should cut several slices before it is passed on to guests.
- Vegetables which are served in a side dish may be eaten with a fork directly from the dish or transferred with your fork or spoon to the dinner plate.

- Edible garnishes which are served with drinks and meals can be eaten, if desired.
- To indicate to a waiter pouring wine that you do not want any, either touch the rim of your wine glass or simply tell the server "No, thank you."
- When coffee cups are turned upside down on their saucers, turn them upright when coffee is being poured to receive coffee service.
- Empty unit-of-use condiment containers or packets should be put on an unused plate. If a plate is not available, butter, jelly or marmalade containers may be placed on, or next to, the butter plate; empty sugar packets should be folded and placed on, under or next to the rim of the coffee cup saucer or butter plate.
- Call the waiter to replace unclean or dropped utensils (do not wipe them off with your napkin) and to clean up spills on the floor.
- Utensils which have been used should not be placed on the dining table. For example, spoons used for soup or to stir iced tea should be placed on the edge of the saucer.
- Requesting a "doggie bag" at the end of a meal may be acceptable on certain social dining occasions, where guests are well known to each other; it is inappropriate, however, when dining with business associates.
- A woman may quickly check her make-up at the table, but neither women nor men should comb or otherwise touch their hair at the dining table.

Receiving the Bill

Upon receiving the check, the host should quickly review it for accuracy and then pay in cash, by credit card, or sign for the check if he has an account at the restaurant. Alternatively, the host may prefer to accept the check away from the table, or he may sign the credit card charge slip in advance of the function and request that the receipt be sent to him the next day—such arrangements should be confirmed with the waiter beforehand. See the Section entitled "Tipping."

Glossary of Foods

The business executive should have a familiarity with food names as they might appear on a menu. The following are a few terms that a person might encounter.

Antipasto	An appetizer dish that may include hard sausages, salted fish, cheeses, olives, peppers, and other vegetables. Served cold.
Au gratin	Made with a lightly browned crust of bread or cracker crumbs and/or grated cheese.
Bisque	Rich, thick shellfish soup.
Boeuf [Fr.]	Beef.
Borsch; Borsht	Russian beet soup, served with sour cream.
Bouillabaisse	A chowder made of two or more kinds of fish.
Bouillon	A clear broth, usually of beef.
Brochette	Skewer-cooked meat or other food.
Canapé	A small, toasted slice of bread spread with minced meat, fish or cheese, and served as an appetizer.
Cannelloni	Tubular pasta stuffed with a variety of fillings, topped with tomato or cheese sauce, and baked.
Caper	A Mediterranean bush, the buds of which are pickled and used to flavor foods.
Capon	A castrated rooster, which renders the flesh tender.
Casserole	A covered baking dish in which food is slowly oven cooked and served. Commonly, it is a pasta-based, one course meal, au gratin, cooked uncovered.
Cayenne	A very hot red pepper.
Ceviche	Raw fish marinated in lime juice with seasonings.
Chutney	A spicy relish.
Compote	Stewed fruits in syrup.
Consummé	A clear, brown stock soup.
Crêpe	A very thin pancake which is rolled up, and sprinkled with sugar and/or contains various fillings.
Croquette	A small, rounded mass of minced meat, fish or vegetables, fried in deep fat until browned.
Crudités Vinaigrette	Raw vegetables that are marinated and topped with French dressing made of vinegar, oil and seasonings.
Cruller	A cake shaped in twisted strips that is made of sweetened dough enriched with eggs; it is deep fat fried until golden brown.
Crumpet	An unsweetened dough baked in muffin rings on a griddle.

Du jour	A food specialty "of the day."
Entrée	The main course of a meal.
Escargots [Fr.]	Snails.
Foie gras	Traditionally, goose liver which is used uncooked or cooked in recipes or as a pâté. Chicken liver may be substituted.
Fricassee	Meat cut into pieces, simmered and/or sautéed, and served in a sauce of its own gravy.
Fritter	A deep fat fried batter, usually containing cooked or uncooked vegetables, meats, fruits or other food.
Gazpacho	A chilled tomato soup made with cucumber and other vegetables, spices, herbs and olive oil.
Glacés	Ices, prepared with a fruit juice/purée, flavoring, or liqueur, with sugar and water.
Guacamole	Mashed avocado, with tomato, onion and seasonings, used as a dip or a spread.
Gumbo	A soup thickened with okra.
Hominy	Dry corn (maize) hulled and ground into a coarse flour for baking, or broken and cooked as a cereal.
Hors d'oeuvre	An appetizer.
Jambalaya	A highly spiced mixture of rice, usually with chicken and ham.
Jambon [Fr.]	Ham.
Jardinière	A garnish made of sliced vegetables.
Kebabs	Skewered meat which has been cut into cubes.
Kipper	A herring (or other fish) cured by salting and drying or smoking.
Kosher	"Clean" meat which is fit for consumption according to the dietary laws of Judaism.
Krumkake	A Scandinavian cookie which consists of a thin wafer that is rolled and stuffed with filling.
Langouste	Crayfish or spiny rock lobster.
Leeks	A mild flavored, cylindrical onion, often used in soup.
London Broil	Broiled flank steak that is thinly sliced.
Lox	A variety of smoked salmon.
Lyonnaise	Prepared with finely sliced onions.
Maigre	A dish prepared in the Lenten style, without meat.
Manicotti	Small pasta squares stuffed with a variety of fillings, topped with sauce, and baked.
Marmalade	A pulpy preserve containing bits of the fruit.
Meringue	Egg whites beaten stiff and mixed with sugar, often used as a topping for pies.
Mincemeat	Either, finely chopped meat; or, a mixture of chopped apples, spices, suet, raisins and other fruits, and possibly meat, used as a pie filling.
Moussaka	An eggplant and lamb casserole originating in Greece.
Mousse	A light, chilled dessert, made of whipped cream, eggs and other ingredients that are sweetened and flavored. A savory mousse is a jellied mousse made from fish, meat or poultry stock.
Mutton	The flesh of grown sheep (cf., lamb).
Newburg	Often containing diced lobster or other seafood, this is a

80　EXECUTIVE ETIQUETTE

	sauce made of egg yolks, cream and wine.
New England Boiled Dinner	A dish consisting of beef, and whole potatoes, onions, carrots, cabbage and other vegetables which are cooked together.
Oeufs [Fr.]	Eggs.
Oysters Rockefeller	Oysters that are covered with a creamed spinach and other ingredient topping, which is then browned.
Parfait	A frozen dessert made of eggs, syrup, flavoring and whipping cream, or ice cream with crushed fruit or syrup, served in a tall, narrow glass.
Pâté	A meat paste.
Poach	To slowly cook in a liquid, just under the boiling point.
Poissons [Fr.]	Fish.
Potages [Fr.]	Soups.
Poulet [Fr.]	Chicken.
Pullet [Fr.]	A young hen.
Purée	Any food prepared with a blender or by straining the boiled pulp through a sieve.
Rarebit	A cheese mixture made with beer or milk that is melted and served over crackers or toast.
Sashimi	Raw seafood, thinly sliced and served chilled.
Sauté	Pan fried quickly in a small amount of very hot fat.
Scallions	An onion with a long leaf and almost bulbless root.
Scalloped	Covered with a sauce and baked in a casserole.
Scampi	Shrimp/prawns cooked with butter and seasonings.
Shallot	A small onion with a garlic-like flavor.
Sorbet [Fr.]	Sherbet.
Soufflé	A light and puffy food that results from the addition of beaten egg whites just prior to baking.
Steak Tartare	Ground raw beef, capped with raw egg yolk, onion, capers, parsley and anchovy.
Sushi	Raw fish, often with steamed rice in bite-size pieces.
Sweetbreads	Usually, cooked veal pancreas or thymus.
Tempura	A food covered with a flour and egg (and possibly beer) batter which is fried in deep fat.
Teriyaki	A soy sauce-based marinade.
Tetrazzini	Macaroni or spaghetti with poultry or fish in a cream and mushroom sauce, baked in a casserole.
Thermidor, Lobster	Cubed lobster in a cream sauce with mustard, sprinkled with cheese and browned; served in the tail shell.
Timbale	A custardlike, seasoned dish made with meat, fish or vegetables, and baked in a small drum-shaped mold.
Veau [Fr.]	Veal.
Velouté	A white sauce made from meat or fish stock that is thickened with flour and butter.
Venison	Meat from a game animal (usually deer).
Vichyssoise	A thick, cream soup of potatoes and onions, served hot or very cold.
Vinaigrette Sauce	A savory sauce made of oil, vinegar, herbs and other condiment ingredients, and used on cold meats.
Volaille [Fr.]	Poultry.

TABLE MANNERS

Table manners are considered a reflection of one's upbringing and, in business, have a significant impact on how others perceive you professionally as well as socially. Table manners should be learned to the extent that they become a natural part of one's behavior, without having to think of the "rules." This Section should be reviewed along with the Sections "Restaurant Dining Manners" and "Table Settings."

Before the Meal

Upon being seated at the table, the napkin should be unfolded (large napkins may remain half folded) and placed on your lap, with two provisos: if the meal is hosted, wait until after the host has begun to place a napkin on his/her lap; and, if grace or an invocation is said, it will normally be done immediately after being seated and your napkin should not be unfolded beforehand. Other than placing the napkin on your lap and taking a sip of water or other beverage, nothing on the table should be disturbed while waiting. If an item (flatware, china, crystal, napkin) in the place service is missing, ask for the item. If an item is unclean, ask for a replacement—do not clean it yourself.

You should sit in the chair with back posture comfortably erect. While at the table, do not fidget (such as drumming the table with your fingers or touching or combing your hair). While waiting for the meal to be served and between courses, hands may be rested in the lap, wrists may be rested on the table edge, or elbows may be placed on the table near the edge.

Service of the Meal

Before or after guests are seated, water glasses are filled. At a hosted dinner, food service begins with the person to the host's right and proceeds, counterclockwise, around the table to the host, who is served last. Normally, courses are placed in front of you by the server from the left side and, except for items on your extreme left, dinnerware is removed from the right side when the course is finished. Diners should pass serving dishes of food and condiments around the table to the right. When an item on the table is out of reach, you should ask the person nearest the item to "Please pass the (item)." Salt and pepper shakers are passed as a set, even when only one of them is requested. At a formal dinner, platters of food are offered to each guest by the server. Guests should use both the serving fork and spoon to transfer a moderate portion of food to their plates (if a piece of toast is underneath, it is transferred with the food). Also take a portion of any vegetables and/or garnishes which accompany an entrée on the platter.

Place a portion of a condiment next to, and not on, the food it is to accompany; gravy and fluid sauces, however, are placed directly on the meat. Foods such as celery and radishes are placed on the butter plate, if one is present. Bread or rolls will usually be served when the soup or an initial course of salad is served. Where there is no butter plate, an *un*buttered bread or roll may be placed on the tablecloth. Although a salad course may be served after the main course, it is more typically served before or with the entrée. If not already on the main course plate or in a small dish near the dinner plate, the server will offer vegetables to each guest from a serving dish. Coffee or tea may be served with the meal, but is more correctly served with, or after, the dessert. If a certain food or wine is not desired, simply tell the server "No, thank you."

When there is foreign material such as hair or an insect in food, bring it to the waiter's attention and have the dish replaced. At a dinner hosted in the home, the material should, if not too unsettling, be removed and the food eaten (otherwise, inform the host).

Wine Service

Wine may be identified as apéritif (appetizer) wines, dinner wines and after-dinner/dessert wines. Apéritif wines are generally fortified, and commonly include the dry sherries and vermouths, or they may be sparkling wines. For the main course, a dry white wine is typically served with fish, a white or light red wine is served with poultry and white meat, and a red wine with wild fowl and red meat. However, it is acceptable to have white or red wine with any food, and serve only one wine (including champagne) as the dinner wine. Dessert wines are generally sweeter and most are fortified, and include sweet sherries, ports, sauternes and sweet champagnes.

White and rosé wines should be served slightly chilled (about 50° F.), red wines at room temperature (about 70° F.) and sparkling wines well chilled. White wines are opened just before use, whereas red wines should be uncorked one-half to one hour before the meal to permit development of its bouquet.

White wine may be served prior to a first course; otherwise, wine is served when food is brought to the table. The host or person who ordered the wine will be given the bottle cork to examine—it should not be dried out or smell corky. A small amount of wine is then poured into the host's wine glass, who may tip the glass slightly to look for bright color and clarity. He should gently swirl the wine in the glass; sniff and then take a sip of wine to make sure it is alright (has not soured). If satisfactory, he nods approval to the server. If the wine is served at a dinner in the home, the host should check the wine *before* it is brought to the table. The server will pour the wine into each diner's wine glass, about half full, beginning with the person to the host's right and continuing counterclockwise around the table until the host is served.

During the Meal

In smaller groups, you should begin eating only after everyone has been served and, if applicable, the host starts. However, you may proceed in larger groups after several guests have been served and it is evident that service will be uneven; if a hosted function, the host should indicate to those already served to begin.

Whether eating American or continental style, only one or two pieces of food are cut at a time for consumption. Food should be brought to your mouth, such that there is minimal bending of your body to meet the fork or spoon. Needless to say, you should chew food with your mouth closed and talk only when your mouth is not full. Remove troublesome food, bones or pits from your mouth with as little notice as possible, by expelling the item onto a spoon or fork or by grasping it with your thumb and index finger; place the item on your plate and cover it with a bit of food, if necessary. Never lick your fingers after using your hands to eat; use your napkin. If food gets lodged in your teeth, excuse yourself from the table and dislodge it in the restroom or wait until the meal is completed; do not use a toothpick or your finger to dislodge food at the table. Small beverage spills may be removed from clothing or the tablecloth by blotting with your napkin; food spills may be removed with a clean piece of flatware. Your napkin, wetted by dipping a corner into your water glass, may then be used to dab the spot.

While eating, the hand/wrist not in use may be rested in your lap or on the table edge, but one's elbows should *not* be on the table. Cover your mouth with the napkin to burp; then quietly say "Excuse me." If about to cough or sneeze, cover your mouth and nose with your handkerchief (if readily available) or napkin. Use only a handkerchief or tissue to blow your nose; if necessary, excuse yourself from the table.

Before dessert is served, the table is cleared of serving dishes, dinnerware and condiments, and the table is crumbed (i.e., the bread crumbs are removed). At a business meal or formal dinner, diners should never hand plates to the waiter unless it is very evident that a particular item on the table cannot be reached.

Occasionally, finger bowls are offered before or after dessert. Normally, the finger bowl with a doily underneath is placed on the dessert plate, with the dessert fork and spoon to each side of the bowl. Dip the fingers of each hand into the bowl and dry them with your napkin. Then, remove the dessert fork and spoon from the plate and place them to the left and right side of the plate, respectively. With both hands, move the finger bowl and doily to a position at the upper left of your place setting.

Toasting

A toast to an important guest or the host can lend a special significance to a meal. Guests should allow the host, a senior executive or the executive who organized the dinner to make the first toast, and this is typically done once the dessert is served and the wine or champagne glasses are filled. A toast should be relatively brief and always on a warm and laudatory note; an injection of humor may impart a "lift" to the toast, as well. The person making the toast should stand and project in a clear voice. Except for more formal occasions, guests can remain seated. At the conclusion of the toast, guests should turn and, looking at the person who was toasted, raise their glass; the person's name may be repeated in unison and a sip of wine is then taken. If your wine/champagne glass is empty or you are not drinking wine, the empty wine glass or glass of water may be raised. The person who is toasted remains seated and does not drink to the toast. After the toast, he should rise to acknowledge the toast with words of thanks.

Consuming Specific Foods

Guidelines follow for a number of foods which can present diners with a challenge in deciding on the proper method for consumption. Also, as a general rule, if in doubt about whether to use your fingers (even when it is otherwise proper), always opt for using a utensil, particularly at a business function or formal dinner.

Artichokes.
Using your fingers, pull a leaf of the artichoke off, dip the pulpy end into the sauce, and pull it through your teeth to remove the food. When the leaves are all removed, the remaining thistled choke is cut away using the fork and knife to reveal the artichoke heart, which is cut into small pieces, dipped in sauce and consumed.

Asparagus.
Asparagus spears (tips) may be eaten with fork and knife, or with the fingers by grasping the base of the stalk. Fingers should only be used if the asparagus is not overly juicy, no sauce is already covering the asparagus and the tough base of the stalk is present.

Bacon.

Use a fork and knife unless the bacon is crisp and relatively free of grease, in which case it may be picked up and eaten with the fingers, if desired.

Bread and Butter.

For bread and rolls, break off a small piece to be consumed and, holding it on the edge of the butter plate, butter that portion. Hot breads such as muffins and rolls should be cut in half and may be entirely buttered before eating; toast should be buttered first, then cut in half.

Celery/Cherry Tomatoes/Olives/Radishes.

These food items are picked up with the fingers. If they are in a salad, however, use a fork.

Chicken and Other Poultry/Fowl.

Chicken meat should first be cut from the bone using the fork and knife, cutting a few morsels at a time. When as much meat as practical has been cut off the bone, personal preference and the formality of the meal will determine whether the chicken pieces can then be picked up with your fingers to nibble off the remaining meat. Fingers should not be used at formal dinners, business luncheons or dinners, and (usually) when poultry other than chicken is served. At less formal occasions, the chicken or other poultry pieces may be picked up to eat, but it is best to observe the host and follow his lead.

Chops.

A fork and knife should be used to eat lamb and pork chops. The center "eye" of meat is first cut from the bone, which is then cut into a few morsels at a time. If there is a paper frill on the end of the bone, it may be grasped with the fingers and, while keeping the chop pressed against the plate, the remaining meat cut away from the bone.

Clams and Oysters, on the Half Shell.
The clam or oyster shell is picked up in one hand and, with the oyster (shellfish) fork, the clam/oyster is lifted out whole from the shell, dipped in sauce and placed whole into the mouth. The shell with any residual juice may then be picked up and poured into the mouth. Oyster crackers may be sprinkled into the sauce and eaten with the fork.

Clams, Steamed.
The opened clam shell is picked up in one hand and, with the fingers of the other hand, the clam is lifted out by its neck. While holding the neck, remove and discard the neck sheath; dip the clam into the broth and then into the melted butter, and place it whole into the mouth. When finished, the clam broth may be drunk from the bowl.

Corn on the Cob.
Corn on the cob should only be served at informal meals. A large ear may be broken or cut in half. Just a few rows at a time should be buttered, salted (and peppered) and eaten. Hold one end of the corn cob at an angle to the plate while buttering it.

Eggs, Soft-Cooked in Shell.
The shell of a soft-cooked egg served in an egg cup is cracked by a horizontal strike with the knife blade, and the top part of the shell removed. The contents, still in the shell, are then seasoned and spooned out.

Fish.
A small fish may be served whole (with head positioned to the left), in which case you must filet it on your plate. Cut the head off (optional) and, while holding the fish with your fork, slit the flank lengthwise from the gill to the tail. Lift and fold back the upper and then the lower portion of flesh. Place the knife tip underneath one end of the backbone and, with the assistance of the fork, gently lift and

remove the skeleton in one piece. Cut and remove the remainder of the fish. The discarded parts are put to the side of the plate or on your butter plate. If lemon juice is desired on the fish, hold and squeeze the lemon wedge with one hand while providing cover for inadvertent squirts with the other hand; poking the lemon wedge with the tines of a fork while squeezing it will also reduce squirting. The fish may be eaten as each filet is readied or after the entire fish has been fileted.

Fruit, Whole Fresh.
If available, the fruit knife should be used to cut and peel fruit. *Apples* and *pears* should be cut in half, then quartered, cored, and peeled if desired; apple and pear quarter pieces may be eaten with the fingers, or cut into small pieces and eaten with a fork. *Apricots* and *peaches* are halved or quartered, respectively, the pit is removed, the fruit is cut into small pieces and eaten with a fork; the peach quarters may be peeled, if desired. *Bananas* are peeled, cut into small pieces and eaten with a fork. *Berries* should already be stemmed and are eaten with a spoon; *strawberries*, however, may be served with their stems intact, in which case the stem is held with the fingers, dipped into powdered sugar if present, and eaten; the stem is returned to the plate. The fingers are used to convey *grapes* to the mouth; seeds are dropped into your cupped hand or grasped by your thumb and index finger for deposit on the plate. A *grapefruit* should already be halved and the internal sections loosened prior to serving; a grapefruit spoon is then used. *Melons* such as cantaloupe or honeydew are cut in half, or into quarters or eighths, the seeds are removed, and the melon is eaten with a spoon or fork (and knife if the rind is present). *Melon balls* are eaten with a spoon. *Oranges* and *tangerines* are peeled before or after being sliced; the individual sections should then be separated by hand and eaten with a fork. A *papaya* is cut in half, the black seeds removed and the fruit eaten with a spoon.

A *pineapple* should be served already peeled and sliced; eat with a fork. *Stewed fruit* is eaten with a spoon; any pits are expelled from your mouth into the spoon and placed on the plate.

Garnishes.
All edible garnishes (such as olives, cherries, orange slices, parsley, watercress) that are served with beverages and food may be eaten.

Lobster.
Lobster claws should first be cracked (this is normally done before being served), the claws twisted off and the meat extracted with a shellfish fork or nut pick. The tail meat is removed in two half portions with the fork and cut into small pieces. Meat is also selectively extracted from the body. Each lobster morsel is dipped in melted butter or mayonnaise sauce and then eaten. Each leg may be broken off with the fingers and the meat sucked out. The green tomalley (liver) and coral or roe (spawn) within the lobster body may also be eaten, if desired.

Potatoes.
A baked potato may be slit lengthwise with a knife and kneaded with the fingers. The potato is broken open into halves with the hands; butter, seasoning and other toppings may then be put on the potato with a fork. The skin may also be eaten. French fried potatoes are eaten with a fork unless the meal is informal, in which case fingers may be used.

Sandwiches.
Sandwiches are eaten with the hands. Thick sandwiches should be cut into quarters first, and any droppings eaten with a fork. Particularly messy sandwiches may be eaten with fork and knife, if desired.

Snails [Escargots].

The snail shell is held using special tongs; if not provided, hold the shell with your fingers. The snail is extracted with a snail fork (if available), shellfish fork, or pick. The snail is dipped whole into the garlic butter and eaten. Any remaining garlic butter may be sopped up with small pieces of bread using a fork.

Spaghetti.

Spaghetti should never be cut. Although some restaurants provide a large spoon for use with a fork, spaghetti is properly eaten only with the fork. A few strands of spaghetti are entwined on the fork tines by turning the fork until all of the strands are wound on. The fork full is then conveyed to your mouth. This process should be done carefully so as not to splatter sauce or have the spaghetti slide off the fork back onto the plate.

TABLE SETTINGS

The business/professional person should be familiar with the placement and use of dining utensils, china and crystal. The ability to correctly set a table when hosting a dinner in the home, to use table service properly, and to display good table manners (see the Sections entitled "Restaurant Dining Manners" and "Table Manners"), is an important part of every businessperson's knowledge base.

A multicourse place setting is depicted in Figure 1, page 94; less formal place settings follow the same pattern, but with fewer items than are shown. The formality of the occasion will guide the selection of the type, quality, colorfulness and proper usage of flatware, china, crystal, condiment servers, napkins, tablecloth, centerpiece and candles. At a formal dinner, flatware should be silver (preferably sterling).

Flatware

Placement.
Flatware is set with the handle ends about one inch from the edge of the table. It is placed on both sides of, and optionally above, the main plate, with forks placed to the left, and knives and spoons to the right. The utensils are arranged in order of use from the outside in, corresponding to the courses of the meal. For example, a salad fork and knife may be located on either side of the dinner fork and knife, depending on when the salad is to be served. The dessert fork and spoon may be placed above the main plate,

as in Figure 1; placed in the inside positions of the forks and spoons; or, brought to the table when dessert is served. With the exception of the optional addition of a small oyster/shellfish fork placed to the right of the spoon(s), there are never more than three forks and/or three knives in a place setting. If another fork or knife is needed, it is placed on the table when the course is served. Note that the knife blades face toward the plate. The butter knife is placed straight, or at a slight diagonal from upper left to lower right, across the top rim of the butter plate, with the blade facing the center of the plate. In formal settings, only the soup spoon is placed to the right of the knives, with a demitasse spoon/teaspoon placed to the right of the coffee cup and saucer. Typically, however, one will find a dessert spoon or teaspoon placed to the immediate right of the knives with the soup spoon, if any, to its right.

Use.
There are two accepted methods for handling a fork and knife, referred to as the American and continental styles. In both styles, the fork is held in your left hand, tines pointing down, to hold the food in place; and the knife is held in your right hand to cut it. In the American style, the knife is returned to the plate and the fork is transferred to the right hand, tines up, to pick up the piece of food. In the continental style, the fork remains in the left hand and, with tines still down, the piece of food is conveyed by fork to your mouth; the knife remains in your right hand, as long as needed. Whichever style is used, when the fork is in the left hand with tines pointing down, the index finger should extend over the shaft; the fork handle should *not* be gripped in the palm of your hand at a 90° angle to the dinner plate (see Figure 2, page 95).

{CONTINUED ON PAGE 95}

94 EXECUTIVE ETIQUETTE

FIGURE 1. MULTICOURSE PLACE SETTING

LEGEND

- A SALAD PLATE
- B BUTTER PLATE
- C BUTTER KNIFE
- D APPETIZER/FISH FORK
- E DINNER/MEAT FORK
- F SALAD FORK
- G SALAD/CHEESE KNIFE
- H DINNER/MEAT KNIFE
- I APPETIZER/FISH KNIFE
- J SOUP SPOON
- K OYSTER/SHELL-FISH FORK
- L SERVICE/DINNER PLATE
- M NAPKIN
- N DESSERT FORK
- O DESSERT SPOON
- P COFFEE CUP & SAUCER
- Q DEMITASSE/TEA SPOON
- R WATER GOBLET
- S RED WINE GLASS
- T WHITE WINE GLASS
- U SHERRY GLASS
- V CHAMPAGNE GLASS
- W PLACE CARD

TABLE SETTINGS 95

FIGURE 2. HOLDING THE FORK PROPERLY

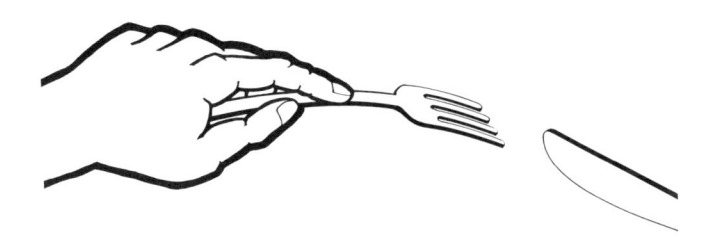

When not in use, a knife is placed diagonally across the upper right edge of the plate, blade facing the center of the plate (see Figure 3). When finished eating, fork and knife are customarily placed together across the middle of the plate from right (handles, slightly over the edge) to left (Figure 3). The knife is placed above the fork, with the blade turned in and fork tines pointing either up or down on the plate.

FIGURE 3. UTENSIL PLACEMENT

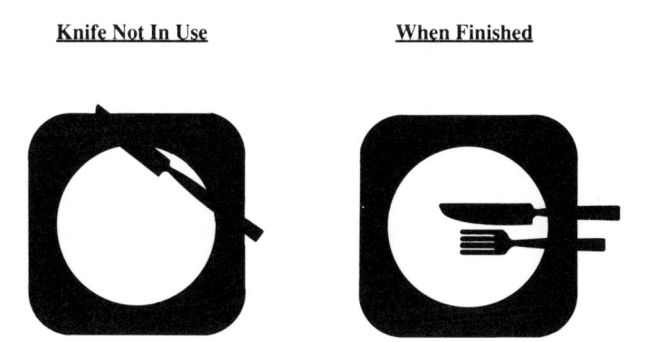

Knife Not In Use   **When Finished**

In using a spoon, soup and other liquids should be spooned away from you. Used spoons are placed on the saucer or underplate of the dish, or may be placed in the dish if it is shallow.

Note that any unused flatware should be left in place on the table, and not put with the used utensils.

China

Placement.
The place setting can include a service plate (also called the place plate, upon which are placed the pre-entrée and dessert course dishes), a dinner plate, salad plate, butter plate, and coffee cup and saucer. The service plate or dinner plate is at the center of the place setting, with all other place setting items arranged around it as shown in Figure 1 (salad plate at the left, butter plate at upper left, and coffee cup and saucer at upper right).

A salad plate will not be on the table when there is a separate salad course, in which case the salad plate is placed in the main plate area when it is served.

Use.
The dishes for the appetizer, soup and/or dessert are placed upon the service or place plate, if one is present. When there is no salad plate and/or butter plate, the dinner plate is used for salad and butter, and the bread/roll may be placed on either the tablecloth (if *un*buttered) or the dinner plate. A bowl may be tipped away from you to spoon out residual liquid.

When serving dishes are passed around the table, you should hold the serving dish so that a handle(s) of the dish and/or of the serving utensil, if present, are readily available for the other diner to grasp.

Crystal

Placement.
Glassware is located above the knives and spoons. Crystal may consist of the water goblet or tumbler, plus other glasses depending on the dinner courses to be served. Other glasses may include, from right to left: a sherry glass (sherry is consumed with certain soups); wine glass (if two are present, one is for white wine which is consumed with a fish course or, absent the sherry glass, with soup, and the other wine glass is for red wine with a meat course); and champagne glass (for the entire dinner or dessert, and toasting).

Use.
A water goblet or other large stem glass is held at the base of its bowl, and a tumbler near its base. A wine glass should be held by its stem to keep the glass unsmudged and help chilled wines remain cool. Your mouth should be empty and lips clean before drinking from crystal to avoid leaving food particles on the rim.

Condiment Servers

Placement.
Condiments should be transferred from their package containers to serving dishes. There should be a salt and pepper set for every one to three diners. Occasionally, salt cellars or pepper pots (small open bowls with spoons), or pepper mills, may be provided instead of shakers.

Use.
Depending on the formality of the meal, condiments will either be offered by a waiter or placed on the table. A small amount of each condiment is placed on your butter or dinner plate, as appropriate, and not directly on the food for which it is intended.

Napkins

Placement.
Cloth napkins, either matched or color coordinated with the table cloth or place mats, should be used. They are usually folded into a rectangle (by folding in half or thirds in each direction to form a square, then folding the two sides, each equal to one-third of the width, over or under) or chevron style (by folding as above into a square, then diagonally in half, and then tucking the pointed ends under). Napkins are placed on the table in the main plate area, or on the service plate if one is utilized. If the first course, such as appetizer or soup, is in place when diners arrive at the table, the napkin is located to the left of the forks. If a monogram is on the napkin, it should be visible.

Use.
Upon being seated at a table, unfold the napkin as much as needed and place it on your lap; if the dinner is hosted, wait until after the host has begun to put a napkin on his lap. In using the napkin, the mouth should be patted or only lightly wiped. At the end of the meal, the napkin is neatly gathered and placed on the table to the left of the place setting, or in the center if plates have been removed.

Place/Menu Cards

At larger functions and/or when guest ranking is necessary, place cards may be used to indicate where individuals are to be seated. Place cards and menu cards, if used, may be handwritten, typed or printed. Place cards are normally white, with or without a gold line border, and up to 3 1/2" wide by 2" high after folding. They are set on the table above the place setting, or on the folded napkin on the service plate. Menu cards are normally white and up to 5" wide by 7" high. They may be set on the table or upright in a holder above each place setting, leaned against the glassware, placed on the folded napkin on the service plate or set on the table between every two diners.

Centerpiece and Candles

A centerpiece comprised of flowers or other decorative arrangement is placed at the middle of the table. The centerpiece should be low enough to permit diners to see over it. If candles are used, one or a pair of candlesticks or a candelabrum is placed at the midpoints between the centerpiece and each end of the table. Candles are normally white or, at less formal occasions, color coordinated with the table linens; they should be of sufficient height that the flame will stay above eye level. The candles are lighted prior to seating diners, and should remain lit until guests have departed from the dining area. Candlesticks are not appropriate for the luncheon table but, if present, should be for decorative purposes only and not lit.

Seating Arrangements

Occasionally, the purpose of the function or the business or professional stature of table guests calls for ranked seating. Figure 4 depicts how chairs should be assigned for the formal business luncheon or dinner, when ranking of guests is involved.

For a formal dinner hosted by husband and wife, the host and hostess sit at opposite ends of the table. If female and male guests are equal in number, seating is alternated female-male along the table, noting that spouses are usually not seated beside each other. Seating is begun with the female guest of honor and next most important female to the host's right and left, respectively, and the male guest of

100 EXECUTIVE ETIQUETTE

honor and next most important male to the hostess' right and left, respectively.

FIGURE 4. RANKED SEATING ASSIGNMENTS

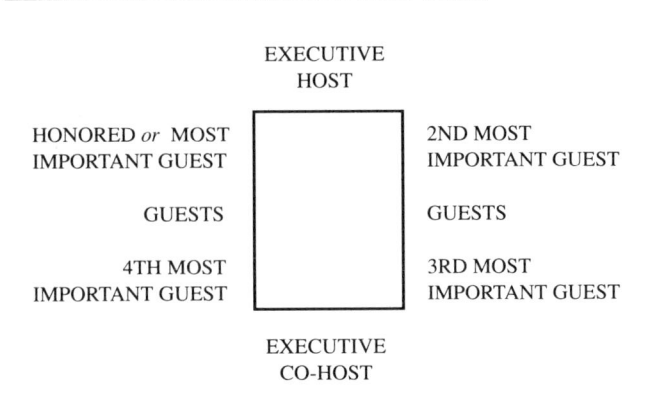

	EXECUTIVE HOST	
HONORED *or* MOST IMPORTANT GUEST		2ND MOST IMPORTANT GUEST
GUESTS		GUESTS
4TH MOST IMPORTANT GUEST		3RD MOST IMPORTANT GUEST
	EXECUTIVE CO-HOST	

For parties of eight or higher multiples of four, all seated at one table, either the host or the hostess may move to the chair on his/her left in order to preserve the alternate female-male seating pattern. Consideration should also be given to seating a left-handed guest at a left corner, in order to prevent elbow bumping with the person to his left.

4 · GIFTS/TRAVEL/COURTESIES

BUSINESS GIFTS

BUSINESS TRAVEL

GENERAL COURTESIES

INTERNATIONAL COURTESIES

Gift giving, travel and common courtesies may involve distinctive features when they relate to business. This Chapter provides guidance on current practices and useful considerations for the businessperson who encounters these areas.

BUSINESS GIFTS

Gift giving is widely practiced in business, involving employers, employees (and perhaps their spouses), customers, clients, and other associates with a business relationship to the firm. Gifts are given on a number of occasions and for various reasons. Business gifts are given to mark such noteworthy business events as a promotion, securing a desired account or closing a major deal; to mark personal milestones and events such as the birth of a child, a birthday, wedding, an illness or retirement; during holiday seasons (primarily Christmas); as an expression of appreciation or friendship; and, as a gesture of goodwill.

Employers have differing policies with respect to employee and corporate gift giving and receiving. It is therefore important that a firm periodically communicate its policies to all employees. Some general guidelines with respect to gifts should be considered.

Giving Office Gifts

- A gift should be appropriate for the recipient and thoughtfully selected. This may require you to learn something about the person's interests and preferences.
- A gift should not be overly expensive, unless the occasion calls for it (such as the retirement of a longtime employee or senior executive). Expensive gifts place undue pressure on others to reciprocate at an equally high level or may send a wrong message to the recipient, who might misconstrue the intentions of the gift giver.

- A gift should neither be too personal or potentially embarrassing to the recipient.
- A gift should be nicely wrapped, and presented with a personalized, handwritten gift card.
- A firm's holiday gifts for staff, if not a standard item, should all have approximately the same value. An executive might choose to also purchase individual gifts for a few persons with whom he/she has worked for a number of years (secretary, administrative assistant, managers).
- A gift of cash or gift having substantial value is more appropriately given jointly by a group of persons within the office.
- Employers and superiors need not give a gift in response to every announcement or invitation received to employees' weddings and other celebratory events. If an invitation is regretted, a warm note of congratulations is sufficient.
- Normally, employees should not, nor are they expected, to give a gift to their superior. Although not required to, an employee may reciprocate an employer's gift with a small gift, but a verbal or written expression of appreciation is customary.
- In order to simplify gift giving in the office, some firms maintain a management fund to purchase cards, gifts or flowers to send on occasions such as an employee's birthday or hospitalization. Offices may also have a gift fund to which the office staff voluntarily contribute a set dollar amount on a regular basis, with rules that specify on which occasions and in what amounts money can be withdrawn for gift giving purposes.

Receiving Office Gifts

- A verbal or written (depending on the occasion) expression of appreciation for a gift should be made. A written thank you note should also be prepared when the gift is

from a group of office staff—this should be sent to the staff, where it can be routed to each contributor or posted on the bulletin board.
- One need not reciprocate the unanticipated business gift from a colleague. A sincere expression of appreciation for the thoughtful gift is acceptable.
- Aside from those occasions when an office staff might pool their resources to present cash or an expensive gift, all inappropriately expensive or personal gifts that could carry the connotation of something more than just business friendship or goodwill should be returned immediately.

Business Associate Gifts

As a method of cultivating goodwill, firms often send promotional items, small special occasion gifts and an annual Christmas holiday gift to their customers and others with a business relationship to the firm. Such items should be carefully selected so as to always reflect quality and a good corporate image. Promotionals usually carry the company logo and are of nominal value. All other business gifts (which may or may not be inscribed with a company logo) should be kept relatively inexpensive. You particularly want to avoid the misconception that a gift is being given as an improper business inducement.

Policies on gift giving and receiving (both the sender's and recipient's firm) should always be learned beforehand, in order to ensure that you take the correct action. Many firms place restrictions on what can be received, to include a prohibition on accepting anything of substantial value.

BUSINESS TRAVEL

Travel is a necessary part of business, government and the professions. The person who knows how to plan a business trip, what to take and how to conduct him/herself makes such trips more productive and easier on oneself and others. The increasing number of women who are joining the ranks of business travelers has also renewed interest in how to handle oneself in various travel situations. Following are some guidelines for business travel.

Preparation

If traveling with colleagues, business schedules and travel arrangements should first be discussed and agreements reached. The business traveler(s) should then ensure that the trip is scheduled and that reservations are made well in advance. This will involve giving information about your appointments, meeting requirements and travel preferences to the travel department/agency or secretary early on. Communicate pertinent plans to the persons being visited, so that any recommended modifications can be made. Prepare a detailed travel itinerary and leave a copy with your office. The itinerary should include information on your transportation, hotel and car rental arrangements, appointments, meeting locations, and telephone numbers where you can be contacted. The interactive nature (with people and systems) of business travel often engenders some amount of stress; therefore, the well prepared executive is one who has also learned to be patient and considerate of others.

In Transit

- Be on time. If traveling by a carrier that requires you to check-in prior to boarding, arrive well before the scheduled departure time.
- Taxi fares, tips and incidental expenses in common should be shared by business persons who are traveling together, unless there has been agreement that one person will pay for and claim such expenses for the group.
- Men and women should carry their own luggage. This does not preclude a woman from requesting, or a man from offering assistance (or vice versa) to carry a burdensome load, where the need is evident.
- Travel light. Storage space is usually limited in cars and corporate aircraft. On commercial aircraft, use clothes racks and overhead compartments first, limiting any carry-on luggage to be stowed under the seat in front of you to one item.
- When traveling with others on short trips, consider using only carry-on luggage (so long as it is not intrusive) in order to avoid having to stop at the luggage claim area.
- When luggage is checked on a commercial airplane, it is recommended that a carry-on always be taken which contains important business papers, basic toiletries and a clean change of clothing, in the event your checked luggage is misrouted.
- When more than two persons are traveling by car or van, the senior person (by age or management level) should be offered the most comfortable seat; normally, this is the front passenger seat. Junior executives should ask where to sit, take a back seat or the least comfortable of available seats (namely, the middle back seat or, in a limousine, the jump seat). This practice should be set aside and the front passenger seat offered to a very large or tall individual, especially when using a compact car.
- While in transit by commercial carrier, consume alcoholic beverages conservatively, if at all. When in cars or

vans, beverages and food should usually not be consumed.
- Be sensitive to the needs and wishes of others with respect to smoking or carrying on a conversation. When traveling by commercial carrier, you may end a conversation with a talkative seatmate by a tactful statement, such as noting how busy you are.
- Whatever conveyance is used, properly dispose of any trash, store reading or other materials, and leave your seat and the surrounding area neat and orderly.
- If there is a delay en route to your business destination, telephone anyone who is waiting for you or expecting you at a certain time. If your itinerary changes, telephone your office.
- You should tip those who provide good service. See the Section entitled "Tipping."

At the Hotel/Dining

- Business colleagues on an expense account who travel together should pay their own expenses (an exception to this might be when a senior executive offers to pay for wine or an entire meal, for example). As a matter of convenience, one person may agree to accept certain bills or pick up restaurant checks and be reimbursed by his colleagues later.
- When hosting a lunch or dinner for others, one person should be designated in advance to take charge of the check.
- Should you dine with the businessperson who you are visiting and he picks up the restaurant check, offer to pay your own amount, but accept if that person is insistent on paying the entire bill.
- Recommendations for women who travel alone:
  - Utilize the hotel's bar, lounges and restaurants; only patronize outside establishments selectively.

- If you accept an invitation to join someone for a drink or dinner in the hotel restaurant, pay your own bill.
  - Carry business notes or a briefcase in a bar or outside restaurant to signal that you are on a business trip.
- Whether dining with colleagues or clients, always use proper table manners (your proficiency at the dining table may, for better or worse, be construed as a reflection of your business competence). See the Sections "Restaurant Dining Manners," "Table Manners," and "Table Settings."
- If you need to conduct business at the hotel and a meeting room is not available, a suite is an acceptable alternative. Use of your own single hotel room should normally be limited to informal business meetings with colleagues, and then only after your room is clean, the bed is made, and all personal items are properly stored.
- Upon arrival at the hotel, bellmen should be tipped at the rate of about one dollar per bag, and one dollar for opening your room. Upon departure, you should leave a tip for the maid service. A general guideline is about one dollar for each night of your stay or two dollars per night in a luxury hotel. For other recommendations on hotel/restaurant tipping, refer to the Section entitled "Tipping."

GENERAL COURTESIES

There are established, common courtesies related to daily living which are also encountered in the course of business. A number of these are rooted in a tradition of deference toward women—such courtesies may continue to be practiced in a social setting. With respect to modern business etiquette, however, men and women should conduct themselves and interact in the same way. Male and female executives should treat other businesspersons, male or female, with equal consideration, for this connotes an honest respect for the individuality of the other person. This does not preclude showing deference to others on occasion, particularly when seniority is the basis.

Anthem/Flag

A person stands quietly (unless singing) throughout the playing of "The Star Spangled Banner" or the national anthem of a foreign country, and anyone walking to their seat (e.g., in a sports arena or theatre) should stop in place during the anthem. Hands are kept at one's sides, and a man wearing a hat should remove it. During the U.S. national anthem, the right hand may be placed over the heart as a further sign of respect (a man wearing a hat would take the hat in the right hand and position it at his left shoulder, with the right hand over his heart).

Essentially the same protocol is followed when the U.S. flag is carried in ceremonial display.

Doors

A man or woman who first reaches a door should open the door, proceed through it and, if others are close behind, hold the door at least partially open until the next person reaches the door handle. If with a group or in deference to a senior person (age or management level), you should remain at the door and continue to hold it open until the other persons pass through it (if the door opens inward, you would wait until the others pass through before going through the door yourself). A man or woman may precede others through a revolving door; however, when the revolving door is not in motion and it is known to be heavy, the considerate executive would go through the door first to exert the force necessary to start it moving.

Elevators

In today's crowded office buildings, elevator etiquette no longer *requires* deferential treatment of women or senior executives. After allowing passengers to disembark, those persons nearest an elevator should enter it first, and move toward the back. If going only a few floors in a high rise building, you should enter after other passengers so that you are situated at the front of the elevator for easier disembarkation.

When disembarking, those at the front of an elevator should exit first (in other words, do not press against others in a crowded elevator in order to let someone at the back disembark before you do). Whoever is within reach should push the "open" button to hold the elevator doors open until passengers have completed exiting and/or entering. Those nearest the elevator doors, if not disembarking, should momentarily step out of the elevator when the doors open, if it will allow persons standing farther back to exit more easily.

112 EXECUTIVE ETIQUETTE

Talking in an elevator should be limited to greeting colleagues and acquaintances. It is strongly advised that personal or business matters not be discussed while in the elevator.

Escalators/Moving Walks

When using an escalator or a moving walk (such as is found in airports), you should stand to the right side to allow other persons to pass, and move to the left side to walk ahead.

Rising/Standing

When other than your co-workers, you should stand and welcome all visitors to your office (including high level company officials and interviewees), and also stand at the end of the meeting and escort visitors to the door. Men seated in a conference room need not rise when a woman enters. This applies also when at a restaurant for a business lunch or dinner; courtesy rather than necessity, however, should govern this situation, and standing when clients or other business associates arrive is a sign of respect that makes good business sense. An executive who is hosting the meal should rise and welcome those who are joining the table, and make the appropriate introductions.

Seating

It is the responsibility of the chairperson of an office meeting or the host of a function to indicate to persons in attendance when and where to be seated. Similarly, those in attendance who are not familiar with customary seating arrangements should wait until the chairperson or host invites them to be seated and/or directs them where to sit. Once seated, always maintain good posture and do not place your feet on a desk or other furniture, even if you are in your own office.

Smoking

Many companies and a number of laws now prohibit smoking in all but designated areas. Further, cigar and pipe smoking may be banned, even when cigarette smoking is permitted. As a visitor to another office, you should refrain from requesting to smoke, unless it is evident (from the presence of ash trays or other persons already smoking) that it is permitted. If permitted, you should inquire of persons near you whether the cigarette smoke will bother them. The smoke from a lighted cigarette should be watched to ensure that it does not drift into someone's face. The cigarette butt should be properly put out and disposed of. Where smoking is allowed, ash trays should be readily available for smokers and the ash trays cleaned regularly. Do not smoke during a meal.

Tipping

Generally speaking, a tip should always be provided for service rendered, with the amount of the tip adjusted to reflect the quality of service. Especially poor or exceptionally fine service should also be reported to the manager. A general schedule of tip amounts is as follows.

In Transit.
Taxi drivers should be tipped approximately fifteen percent of the fare. At an airport, skycaps may be given fifty cents to one dollar per bag for curbside checking of your luggage. Skycaps should be given fifty cents (one dollar minimum) to one dollar per bag when transporting your lug-

gage, and three or more dollars to transport a cart load of luggage.

Hotel.
Upon arrival at a hotel, a doorman may be tipped for bringing your luggage to the reservation desk at the rate of fifty cents (one dollar minimum) to one dollar per bag. The bellman who shows you to your room should be tipped one dollar per bag plus one dollar for opening your room. During your stay, a concierge who has been particularly helpful may be tipped (the amount is highly variable, depending upon how much assistance was provided). The doorman who summons a taxi should receive fifty cents to one dollar; and the parking attendant who parks and retrieves your car one to five dollars per day, depending on how often you use the car during the day.

You may also want to tip the headwaiter if you plan to regularly use the hotel's dining room. Upon departure, you should leave a tip for the maid service of about one dollar for each night of your stay or two dollars per night in a luxury hotel—this may be given directly to the maid, left in a clearly marked envelope in the room, left at the reservation desk, or added to your bill.

Restaurant.
Fifteen percent of the bar bill (fifty cents minimum) is given to the bar server or bartender. Fifteen percent of the total meal bill is the standard tip in most restaurants, and twenty percent (divided into 75% for the waiter and 25% for the captain of your table) in very expensive establishments. The tip may be left on the table or added to the credit card charge slip. Two to five dollars per bottle of wine, or fifteen percent of the wine bill in expensive establishments, is given to the wine steward (sommelier). Upon leaving the restaurant, the headwaiter should also be given up to five dollars if he provided a special service to you. The coatroom attendant

and the doorman who summons a taxi should each be given from fifty cents to one dollar; for valet parking, the attendant should receive from fifty cents to two dollars, depending on the restaurant.

Walking

When a man and woman are on a sidewalk, the man may walk on either side of the woman. However, it is customary for a man to either walk on a woman's left or on the outside of the sidewalk. In the latter case, the man need not repeatedly change sides if several streets are crossed which alter the direction of the walk. Generally, when a man and woman must walk in single file (such as when walking to a table in a restaurant), the woman should precede the man.

INTERNATIONAL COURTESIES

Foreign investment in the United States will likely continue to advance in coming years. This, and the increasing trend of U.S. firms to form business alliances with companies in other parts of the world, has led to an influx of foreign businesspersons to the U.S. These people are often fluent in English and very knowledgeable about our culture. In contrast, their U.S. counterparts usually know comparatively little about the foreigners' countries and relatively few are conversant in other languages.

Americans need to be more informed about, and sensitized to, foreigners' backgrounds, in order to derive as much as possible from their business and social interactions. U.S. businesses with offices abroad should invest in cross-cultural training for their staff. This Section provides basic guidance for the executive who works with foreign businesspersons assigned to this country, with an emphasis on the Japanese.

General Considerations

The first step that the U.S. businessperson can take is to read about the foreign businessperson's country of origin. One should learn key points about the country's geography, political leadership, historical milestones, major export and import items, cultural heritage, sociological characteristics and principal religious observances. Further, learn a few words and phrases in the other person's language which might be used in daily conversation.

The foreigner stationed in the U.S. will likely adapt to American ways of doing business. However, it is in the interest of U.S. businesspersons to be aware of how business is practiced in other countries, particularly where there may be significant differences. This will reduce the chance of a gaffe which could undermine business discussions. A few examples of differing practices are provided here.

- Greetings and Introductions. Americans tend to be expressive and open in their greetings. In cultures such as the Chinese, Japanese and in many European countries, however, people are more reserved—embraces or touching would be considered inappropriate, and titles are often retained even after individuals know one another.
- Conducting Business. U.S. business generally involves an approach that is assertive and direct. In many countries, however, business is transacted with more deliberation and subtlety. Further, foreign business is often conducted with the intent of forming long-term relationships.
- Forms of Behavior. Occasionally, an innocuous practice in the U.S. may be inappropriate in other countries. For example, in Arab countries, one does not use the left hand to hold, give or receive items; when sitting, the soles of the shoes should not be visible to others; and, in certain countries, business is not conducted on Fridays (the Islamic holy day).
- Gifts. Business gift giving is even more a custom in some foreign countries than in the U.S., and businesspersons here should not be surprised to receive a small gift from foreigners.

U.S. business could garner much good will by adopting some of the practices that foreign businesspersons bring to this country, and Americans would do well to take the opportunity to learn from them.

Japanese Business Style

Because of the very substantial economic presence of the Japanese in the U.S., a brief review of their approach to business follows.

Doing business with the Japanese is made easier with a knowledge of the attitudes and customs which shape their lives. Basically, the Japanese businessperson strives for harmony with his co-workers and those he deals with. Business is typically a life-long commitment and the company becomes a "family" for its employees. Loyalty and the common good are emphasized, and mutual respect and trust are encouraged between staff and management.

There is a need for the Japanese to feel "amae," or a complete trust and dependence on others. It takes time for a Japanese businessperson to feel this sense of trust with others. The U.S. businessperson needs, therefore, to work at instilling this confidence at a personal level in the business relationship.

The Japanese often arrive at business decisions by consensus. Japanese executives have a high sense of devotion to their company and work within the team framework, with each person having a "station" within the organization. In many cases, an individual cannot make decisions or commitments independently. U.S. businesspersons need to have patience and understanding during this decision-making process. If an interpreter is utilized, that person should have significant business experience and be very familiar with the "Japanese way" of transacting business.

Most Japanese businesspersons are university graduates and are considered an elite group within their country. As with businesspersons from any foreign country, they should be accorded due respect.

5 · PERSONAL GROOMING & BUSINESS DRESS

GENERAL CONSIDERATIONS

ATTIRE FOR WOMEN

ATTIRE FOR MEN

ATTIRE FOR VIDEO

In business, a professional as well as personal statement is made by one's grooming and dress. The businessperson's appearance projects an image to others which can significantly impact their perceptions. This Chapter provides guidance on good personal grooming and appropriate attire for business.

PERSONAL GROOMING & BUSINESS DRESS

Your appearance has a significant, and sometimes a determinant, impact on how others perceive you as a person and your competence as a professional. You should always be aware that your appearance is projecting a personal, professional and corporate *image,* and therein lies its importance in the business world. Aside from physical characteristics, your appearance is enhanced by good grooming and attire that is both stylish and properly fitted. This will signal to colleagues and clients that you care about yourself and this, in turn, transfers to caring about your firm and the products and services it produces. Giving such attention to oneself often has the added benefit of producing a psychological lift which is reflected in your countenance.

General Considerations

Grooming.
The importance of good grooming habits for women and men in business should not be undervalued—good grooming is fundamental to a pleasing appearance. Although aspects of it are self evident, good personal grooming includes the following. Always bathe and use a deodorant daily. Your hair should be clean, dandruff-free and neatly combed or brushed; keep it trimmed. For men, the face is well-shaven and/or facial hair is neatly trimmed. Hands should be clean and finger nails meticulously clean and trimmed. Good oral hygiene should be evident, to include regular brushing of the teeth.

Fragrances should be understated and used very sparingly. Women should apply makeup carefully and sparingly.

An essential part of grooming is ensuring that clothes and accessories are clean and well maintained. Clothing (including the necktie, bow or scarf) should be clean and pressed—this requires regular professional laundering and dry cleaning. One should check over clothing for loose threads, loose or missing buttons, loose seams and tears. Belts, shoes and other leather accessories should be clean, polished and in good repair. Handkerchiefs should be clean.

Clothing.
Attire for business people is predominantly conservative, but dress standards vary according to the nature of one's profession. For example, attorneys generally dress very conservatively, whereas those in advertising or high technology fields often have some latitude in what can be appropriately worn. The geographic location of the firm, company standards and office milieu also influence what constitutes acceptable dress, and all of these factors combine to form a "dress code" that is in effect. You should always take the dress code into account when selecting your wardrobe, and stay within it as much as possible.

Conventional business attire is normally worn at a function such as a business-related cocktail or dinner party. A sports jacket for men and party dress for women may be alternatives for a cocktail party. If you are uncertain about what to wear, always contact the host beforehand so as not to appear out of place at the function.

In business clothing, as in other areas, fashion trends are cyclical, but classic cuts are almost always in style. Fashionably stylish apparel is fine as long as it is neither extreme nor faddish. Fabric pattern and color should generally be understated, in darker shades and muted tones. Accept only quality fabric, which is durable and holds its shape. Made-to-measure suits and shirts are usually superior, but most people wear off-the-rack clothing which is quite acceptable if it is a quality product and the tailoring is well done. The fit of apparel may change over time, and should be adjusted as necessary. Always have your clothes altered when you have a noticeable weight loss or gain. Consistency of dress is also important—do not appear at the office in stylish looking apparel some days and inexpensive or outdated looking attire at other times, because of the "incongruent" impression it presents.

Office Grooming Kit.
A kit should be maintained at your office which contains an assortment of grooming products. The kit should include the following items, many of which can be found prepackaged in a travel kit or purchased individually in small product sizes: a mirror; comb or hair brush; hair spray; makeup (for women); shaving gel and razor (for men); nail clipper/file; toothbrush and toothpaste; fragrance; handkerchief; lint brush; shoe polish and brush; and sewing items.

Attire for Women

Businesswear.
At the office or for a business lunch, dinner or party, a suit with matching skirt and jacket is the most effective attire for women. The blouse should be color coordinated and may be plain front or minimally ruffled. The blouse can be accessorized with a bow, complementary scarf or a tasteful neckchain or necklace. A conservative dress with coordinating jacket, or a dress or skirt with blazer are good alternatives to the suit. Though somewhat variable depending on one's height, the dress or skirt hemline should normally fall to a position slightly below the knees. Avoid low necklines or blouses too open, short skirts or overly tight clothing.

Wool or wool blends and textured cotton/polyester blends are among the best fabrics in terms of their appearance and wear properties. The best solid colors for women's business attire include blues, grays, browns, beige and occasionally black. Solid colors are best, but subtle plaids and tweeds are good alternatives. Pantsuits are seldom seen in business, although they are acceptable in some settings if they are well tailored and have a quality appearance.

Hosiery/Shoes.
Hosiery should be limited to plain, skin-toned pantyhose. Conservative pumps and other low or medium heel, closed shoes are proper business wear. Boots are not acceptable footwear in most offices.

Accessories/Jewelry.
Accessories should always be integrated into an overall look. Belts and belt buckles should be stylish, but not distracting. Similarly, jewelry is appropriate when it is tastefully stylish, but not so much or so loud that it draws attention away from you or the business at hand. Only wear an excellent quality watch that is conservatively stylish. Purses and handbags should be coordinated with your clothing and shoes, but, again, should be "minimal." Only quality pens and pocket calendars should be used.

Attire for Men

Suits.
At the office, for a business lunch, dinner or party, the business suit is the proper attire for men. In certain offices and locales, the classic navy or camel hair blazer or tweed jacket with complementary slacks may also be acceptable, as are seersucker or poplin suits during the summer. For business dinners or parties in the home, the business suit or a sports jacket (with or without a tie, depending on the formality of the function) and slacks are appropriate.

There are several factors to consider in purchasing a suit. The suit should generally have a traditional cut. A medium width lapel is currently in style, and shirt collars and neckties should be of corresponding width. Sleeve length should allow one-quarter to one-half inch of the shirt cuff to show. Wool or wool blends are among the best fabrics in terms of their appearance and wear properties. It is generally accepted that the best suit colors for men are dark blues, charcoal, grays, dark browns and beige. Dark solids are always in style. Pinstriping should be understated (avoid chalk stripes), and plaids intricate and understated. A more authoritative look may be achieved when the suit is darker in color, and this should be considered for so-called "power" meetings. Aside from the quality of the suit, proper fit is the most important consideration, and a good tailor is essential.

Shirts.
Business shirts should always be long sleeved (which, within the confines of your office, can be rolled up) and pockets should be limited to one, located over the left breast. Collars may be plain point with stays, button-down (less formal) or made for a collar pin. Because of the high degree of variability in ready-made shirts, make certain that the fit is proportional to your body shape and size. The optimum fabric is a high content cotton blend, which combines the inherent wearability of cotton with the wrinkle resistance of a synthetic fiber. Solid whites and certain pastel shades are always acceptable colors, as are narrow, defined stripes on a solid white or pastel colored background.

Neckties.
Medium width neckties are currently in style. Neckties should be made of a good quality fabric such as silk or a silk blend. Your wardrobe may also include a few finely woven wool ties, as well. Neckties should be relatively

conservative in design, and design/color coordinated with the shirt and suit. They should be worn such that the tip reaches to the belt, with the tail placed through the tab on the backside of the necktie (this is in lieu of a tie clip or tie pin, which are presently not in style). Bow ties are often looked upon as the mark of an individualistic personality, and this should be considered in deciding to wear them.

Underwear/Socks/Shoes.
When wearing a dress shirt with the collar open at the neck, the undershirt should not show. Socks should be over-the-calf in length, and of such quality that they stay in place. With respect to color, dark brown socks are worn with brown suits, and dark blue, dark gray or black socks are worn with all other suits. Similarly, brown shoes are worn with brown or khaki-colored suits, and black or cordovan shoes are worn with all other suits. Laced shoes are standard business footwear, although dress loafers have gained acceptance in recent years. Boot-styled shoes are not accepted office footwear. It is recommended that a pair of shoes not be worn on consecutive days—they should be allowed to air out and shoe trees utilized to maintain their shape.

Accessories/Jewelry.
Accessories and jewelry should be kept to a minimum. Belt buckles and cuff links should be conservative in appearance. A white handkerchief may properly be placed in the suit breast pocket, a portion of which is displayed. Limit rings to your wedding band, plus a collegiate or signet ring if it is conservative in design and size. Only wear an excellent quality watch that is conservatively stylish. The contents of your billfold should be kept to a minimum so that it is not bulky in your pants or coat pocket; pocket coins, also, should be kept to a minimum; and keys should be enclosed in a flat key case. Only quality pens and pocket calendars should be used.

Attire for Video

With increasing regularity, businesses are relying on closed circuit and public telecasts, live or taped, to convey their message. Typically, a camera focuses in on the spokesperson, resulting in an accentuation of his personal appearance. Set lighting and background significantly impact on this visual image, including what the person is wearing. Attire should therefore be selected with care—a few guidelines follow.

- Learn beforehand what color of backdrop will be used, so that a complementary, yet contrasting color of clothing can be selected.
- Solid colored shirts, principally white and pastel colors, work best on camera. Color distortions can occur when there are intricate patterns or narrow stripes, so these should be avoided.
- Neckties should complement the shirt in a contrasting color that is devoid of complex patterns or narrow, bright-colored stripes.
- Suits in solid colors or with muted pinstripes are the safest; avoid small checks and plaids.
- Do not wear any jewelry that could jingle or easily reflect the lighting on the set.
- Just prior to air time, a light powder makeup should be applied to those areas of the head—the nose, upper forehead and bald areas—that have a tendency to shine under set lighting.
- Do a test videotape which can be reviewed on a monitor in advance of the real session.

INDEX

Address, Forms of, 31-35
    Government officials, 31
    Military personnel, 32
    Professional persons, 33
    Religious persons, 34
Addressing Others, 27, 31
Air Travel, 107-108
Answering the Telephone, 47
Anthem Etiquette, 110
Appearance,
    See Business Dress
Appointments
    Job interviews, 60
    Office, 59
    Offsite, 60
Attire for Business,
    See Business Dress
Automobile Travel, 107-108

Board of Directors
    Meetings, 64
Business Cards, 3-5
    Design, 3
    Purpose, 4
    Specifications, 3
    Use, 5
Business Correspondence, 6-22
    Appearance, 7
    Business documents, 6
    Composition, 6
    Letter elements, 9
    Letter formats, 15
    Letters of reference, 19
    Memoranda, 20
    Purpose, 6
    Stationery, 8
Business Documents, *See* Business Correspondence
Business Dress, 119-127
    Attire for men, 124
    Attire for video, 127
    Attire for women, 123
    General considerations, 121
Business Entertaining,
    See Dining/Entertaining
Business Gifts, 103-105
    Business associate gifts, 105
    Giving office gifts, 103
    Receiving office gifts, 104
Business Letters, Elements
    Attention line, 10
    Closing data, 13
    Complimentary close, 12
    Date line, 9
    Declarations/notations, 9
    Envelope address, 13
    Inside address, 9
    Salutation, 10
    Signature block, 12
    Subject line, 10
    Text, 11
Business Letters, Formats
    Executive letter form, 17
    Full block form, 15
    Inserting into envelope, 19
    Modified block form, 15
    Modified semiblock, 16
    Punctuation, 17
    Simplified form, 17
Business Travel, 106-109
    Dining, 108
    At the hotel, 108
    Preparation, 106
    In transit, 107

Cards
    Business, 3
    Menu, 98
    Place, 98

Chairing a Meeting, *See*
    Meetings/Conferences
China [Dining], 96
Cigar/Cigarettes,
    See Smoking Etiquette
Clergy
    Forms of address, 34
Cocktail Functions, 69-72
    Attire, 122
    Guest considerations, 71
    Host considerations, 69
Communications, 1-50
    Business cards, 3
    Business correspondence, 6
    Conversation, 23
    Greetings & introductions, 27
    Invitations & replies, 36
    Presentations/speaking, 43
    Telecommunication, 47
Conferences, *See*
    Meetings/Conferences
Consuming Beverages
    At a party, 71
    In a toast, 85
    Wine service, 83
Consuming Food
    American style, 84
    Continental style, 84
    Glossary of foods, 78
    Manners, 84
    At a party, 72
    At a restaurant, 76
    Specific foods, 86
Conversation, 23-26
    Effective listening, 25
    Effective speaking, 25
    At a party, 72
    At a restaurant, 76
    Telephone, 49
    What to say, 24
Correspondence, *See*
    Business Correspondence
Courtesies, *See*
    General Courtesies *and*
    International Courtesies
Crystal, 97

Dining/Entertaining, 67-100
    Cocktail functions, 69
    Restaurant dining
      manners, 73
    Table manners, 81
    Table settings, 92
Door Etiquette, 111
Dressing for Business,
    See Business Dress

Eating,
    See Consuming Food
Elevator Etiquette, 111
Entertaining,
    See Dining/Entertaining
Envelopes
    Addressing, 8, 13
    Inserting letter, 19
    Mailing invitations, 40
    Size, 8
Escalator Etiquette, 112

Flag Etiquette, 110
Flatware, 92
Food
    Consuming specific
      foods, 86
    Glossary of foods, 78
    Restaurant ordering, 75
    See also Consuming Food
Foreign Businesspersons, *See*
    International Courtesies
Forms of Address, 31-35
    Government officials, 31
    Military personnel, 32
    Professional persons, 33
    Religious persons, 34

General Courtesies, 110-115
    Anthem/flag, 110
    Doors, 111

INDEX 131

Elevators, 111
Escalators, 112
Moving walks, 112
Rising/standing, 112
Seating, 112
Smoking, 113
Tipping, 113
Walking, 115
Gifts,
See Business Gifts
Gifts/Travel/Courtesies,
101-118
Business gifts, 103
Business travel, 106
General courtesies, 110
International courtesies,
116
Glossary of Foods, 78
Government Officials
Forms of address, 31
Greetings, *See*
Greetings & Introductions
Greetings & Introductions,
27-35
Addressing others, 27
Forms of address, 31
Greetings, 28
Introductions, 29
Grooming,
See Personal Grooming
Guest Responsibilities
Bringing a guest, 42
Cancelling an acceptance,
41
At a cocktail function, 71
Inviting a superior, 42
Reciprocating an invitation,
42
Replies to invitations, 41
Thank yous, 42

Handshake
In greeting, 28
At job interview, 61
At office appointment, 59

Hat, During anthem, 110
Host Responsibilities
At a cocktail function, 69
At a meeting, 59
At a restaurant, 73-78

International Courtesies,
116-118
General considerations, 116
Japanese business style, 118
Interoffice Memoranda,
See Memoranda
Interpreter of Japanese, 118
Interviewing for a Job, 60
Introductions, *See*
Greetings & Introductions
Invitations & Replies,
36-42
Content, 37
Invitations, 36
Mailing, 40
Replies, 41
Responsibilities, 41
Types, 36

Japanese Business Style, 118
Jewelry/Accessories
For men, 126, 127
For women, 124, 127
Job Interviews, 60
Interviewee, 61
Interviewer, 61
Résumé, 62

Letterhead, 8
Letters, *See*
Business Correspondence
Letters of Reference, 19
Listening
Conversational, 25
At a meeting, 58

Meetings/Conferences,
51-66
Board of directors, 64

132 INDEX

The chairperson, 53
Conferences, 65
Job interviews, 60
Meeting notes, 55
Office appointments, 59
Offsite appointments, 60
The participants, 57
Résumé, 62
Meeting Notes, 55
Meeting Room, 54, 109
Memoranda
Appearance, 20
Elements, 20
Format, 21
Types, 21
Menu Cards, 98
Menu Items, defined, 78-80
Military Personnel
Forms of address, 32
Officer ranks, 33
Minutes of Meeting, 55
Moving Walk Etiquette, 112

Name Badges, 71
Names
Addressing others, 27-28
On business cards, 3-5
On business letters, 9-18
On envelopes, 8, 13
In introductions, 29-30
On invitations, 38-41
In meeting notes, 56
On memoranda, 20-22
On stationery, 8
On the telephone, 47-49
Napkins, 98
National Anthem, 110
Neckties, 125, 127

Parties,
See Cocktail Functions
Personal Grooming, 119-127
Place Cards, 98
Place Setting,
See Table Settings

Presentations/Speaking,
43-46
Conversational, 24-25
Delivery, 44
Introducing the speaker, 46
At a meeting, 57-58
Preparation, 43
Stage presence, 46
Professional Persons
Forms of address, 33
Promotional Items, 105
Public Speaking, *See*
Presentations/Speaking

Reference Letters, 19
Religious Persons
Forms of address, 34
Replies [to Invitations], *See*
Invitations & Replies
Reservations
At a restaurant, 73
Restaurant Dining Manners,
73-80
Arrival and seating, 74
Conversation, 76
Eating, 76
Glossary of foods, 78
Menu items, 78
Ordering, 75
Receiving the bill, 77
Reservations, 73
While traveling, 108
Résumé, Preparing a, 62
Rising/Standing, 112
Robert's Rules of Order, 65
R.S.V.P.'s, *See*
Invitations & Replies

Seating
At a dining table, 99
Etiquette, 112
At a meeting, 57
At a restaurant, 74
Seminars,
See Meetings/Conferences

INDEX

Shirts/Blouses
    For men, 125, 127
    For women, 123, 127
Shoes
    For men, 126
    For women, 124
Silverware, 92
Smoking Etiquette, 112
Socks/Hosiery
    For men, 126
    For women, 124
Speaking, *See*
    Presentations/Speaking
Standing/Rising, 112
Stationery
    Envelopes, 8
    Letterhead, 8
Suits
    For men, 124, 127
    For women, 123, 127

Table Manners, 81-91
    Before the meal, 81
    Consuming specific foods, 86
    During the meal, 84
    Service of the meal, 82
    Toasting, 85
    Wine service, 83
Table Settings, 92-100
    Candles, 99
    Centerpiece, 99
    China, 96
    Condiment servers, 97
    Crystal, 97
    Flatware, 92
    Menu cards, 98
    Napkins, 98
    Place cards, 98
    Seating arrangements, 99

Telecommunication, 47-50
    Additional guidelines, 50
    Answering the telephone, 47
    Placing a call, 49
    Telephone conversation, 49
Telephone Etiquette,
    See Telecommunication
Tipping/Tips
    Hotel, 114
    Restaurant, 114
    In transit, 113
Titles
    On business cards, 4
    On envelopes, 13
    Greetings/introductions, 27-35
    In international business, 117
    In letter inside address, 9
    In letter salutation, 10
    In letter signature block, 12
    In letter text, 11
    In memoranda, 21
Toasting, 85
Travel,
    See Business Travel

Video, Attire for, 127
Voice
    Delivery in speaking, 44
    Effective speaking, 25

Walking Etiquette, 115
Wardrobe
    See Business Dress
Wine
    Restaurant ordering, 75
    Service at table, 83